M000096775

To

JUSTIN,

BLESSINGS FOR

WISDOM & FOR

WEALTH!

From

Wisdom Before Wealth

Wisdom Before Wealth

*Principles of Wealth Creation and Financial Independence
for the Next Generation*

RANDALL P. SANADA,
CFP,® CKA®

You shall teach them to your children …
when you are walking by the way…
— *Deuteronomy 11:19 (ESV)*

EQUIP PRESS
Colorado Springs, Colorado

Wisdom Before Wealth

Copyright © 2017 by **Randall P. Sanada**

All rights reserved. No part of this publication may be reproduced, distributed, or transmitted in any form or by any means, without prior written permission.

Scripture quotations marked (ESV) are taken from The ESV® Bible (The Holy Bible, English Standard Version®) copyright © 2001 by Crossway, a publishing ministry of Good News Publishers. ESV® Text Edition: 2011. The ESV® text has been reproduced in cooperation with and by permission of Good News Publishers. Unauthorized reproduction of this publication is prohibited. Used by permission. All rights reserved.

Scripture quotations marked (KJV) are taken from the King James Bible. Accessed on Bible Gateway at www.BibleGateway.com.

Scripture quotations marked (NASB) are taken from the New American Standard Bible ® (NASB), copyright © 1960, 1962, 1963, 1968, 1971, 1972, 1973, 1975, 1977, 1995 by The Lockman Foundation, www.Lockman.org. Used by permission.

Scripture quotations marked (NIV) are taken from the Holy Bible, New International Version. Copyright © 1973, 1978, 1984, 2011 by Biblica, Inc.® Used by permission. All rights reserved worldwide.

Scripture quotations marked (NKJV) are taken from the New King James Version®. Copyright © 1982 by Thomas Nelson, Inc. Used by permission. All rights reserved.

Scripture quotations marked (NLT) are taken from the Holy Bible, New Living Translation, copyright © 1996, 2004, 2015 by Tyndale House Foundation. Used by permission of Tyndale House Publishers, Inc., Carol Stream, Illinois 60188. All rights reserved.

Scripture quotations marked (NRSV) are taken from the New Revised Standard Version Bible, copyright © 1989 the Division of Christian Education of the National Council of the Churches of Christ in the United States of America. Used by permission. All rights reserved.

First edition 2017

Wisdom Before Wealth / Randall P. Sanada
ISBN-13: 978-1-946453-04-4

DEDICATION

I'd like to dedicate this book to my wife, Kay, and our four incredible sons, Randy Jr., Jerry, Chad, and Joe. In this book, I discuss the disciplines of wealth creation and share stories from my journey of discovery and implementation of these financial principles. Without the support and cooperation of my wife, Kay, the implementation part would have been impossible. Multiple times we struggled together (and sometimes against one another) with the discipline of deferred gratification. How much more fun it would have been at the time to go ahead and buy that new furniture on credit as our friends were doing. How enjoyable it would have been to stay in fine hotels rather than camping during our early vacations (which turned out to be great fun anyway). It wasn't easy for her, but Kay stuck with me and my frugal ways during those early years. Hopefully today she agrees that it was all worth it!

Our sons also had to learn about stewardship disciplines and were required to develop a work ethic early on. It was difficult to see Randy Jr.'s disappointment when there wasn't a new car in the driveway for him on his sixteenth birthday, despite the fact that by then we had the funds to purchase one for him if we had so chosen. Instead, he and his brothers were required to earn the funds for the purchase of their cars. They took good care of those cars too; after all, they had "skin in the game." Together we devised a plan for them to pay for their own college educations. They each pulled it off and earned excellent grades along the way.

And as you might imagine, they didn't stop their journeys of excellence there. As adults now, they have each achieved great success, professionally, financially, and, most importantly, as stalwart, godly men. I have every confidence that they will raise their families better than I did mine. How I wish I could take all of the credit for their successes, but the reality is that with God's help, they each succeeded through self-discipline.

Today, Randy Jr. and Jerry run our multi-family offices. They oversee most of our investments (and the associated financial services firms) for the benefit of our family and the families we serve. I am rarely present in meetings with clients anymore; they have full confidence in my sons and their team of financial advisors. Chad is a chemical engineer and has achieved great success in his profession, while we affectionately refer to Joe as a recovering attorney. Today, Joe and his wife operate companies in the wedding photography business.

I wrote this book in part to commemorate our family's financial journey, but more importantly to equip you, my sons, with a written resource to pass down the principles that you have applied so aptly to your own lives. Thank you, my family—my team; with God's help, we did it together. You have blessed me in so many ways, and I am so very proud of you! You are cherished in my heart.

ACKNOWLEDGMENTS

I would like to acknowledge and thank everyone who has helped, influenced, and inspired me to make this book a reality:

My grandparents and my parents

My wife and sons

Family & Friends: Kathy Saigeon, Judy Smith and Leigh Anne Tsuji

Mentors: Ron Blue, Larry Burkett and Howard Dayton

My staff and associates: including Rick Farwell, Jon Rehurek and Chase Western

Pastors: Francis Chan, Sam Gallucci, Ron Prinzing and Larry Reichardt

Fellow authors: Caleb Breakey, Loran Graham, Darrell Griffin and Adam Swiger

CONTENTS

A LETTER TO OUR GRANDCHILDREN

This book is intended for a relatively wide audience. It started out as an extended letter to my grandchildren who will soon be young adults. I've also written it so that others can impart these principles to their own children, grandchildren, nephews and nieces. My hope is that the book will be given as a gift to future generations, hence the To/From page in the front. It's rare for young people to receive any meaningful financial training. Not from their parents, not from schools—not really from anywhere. I've enjoyed a wonderful financial journey, thanks in part to the principles my grandparents shared with me at a very early age.

It's not easy to capture the attention of young people, given their busy lives so full of activities and entertainment. However, it happens that I did find a way to do this while skiing with my sons. There were regular moments when they were a captive audience—while we were on the chairlift together. It was there they learned about compound interest and Formula 15 for financial independence. With a little ingenuity, you can find a way to give your children or grandchildren a head start on their own financial journeys.

Finally, a desire of my heart is that this book be of assistance to fellow financial advisors as a tool to help prepare their clients for the counsel they will be receiving. The reader is first exposed to the very simple principles of compound interest and then introduced to the concept of financial independence. Then in building block fashion, the reader is presented with advanced methods of enhanced investment returns and risk reduction, and finally the achievement of true financial freedom.

A Letter to My Grandchildren

And now to my precious grandchildren (Ryan, Jacob, Paul & Kate):

I love you. You already know that, but my love for you is of a magnitude that you cannot yet comprehend. Only when you are grandparents will you understand and appreciate this kind of love. I was blessed to have been raised in a Christian home with both a mom and dad who loved me unconditionally, and with grandparents who exclaimed their love for my siblings and me beyond our comprehension. Experiencing this kind of love enabled me to better understand God's unconditional love for me, and was foundational to my identity. It's my hope that you will recognize the precious wealth that you possess in this unconditional love from your grandparents, parents, and siblings, and that you will carry this knowledge through your lifetimes.

It is also my hope that this book will impart some basic principles founded in biblical wisdom that will better equip you for the management of the finances God may entrust to you.

A good man leaves an inheritance to his children's children. — ***Proverbs 13:22 (ESV)***

It's also my hope and expectation that you will receive a good inheritance. Money is probably the first thought that comes to mind when you imagine an inheritance. And while, yes, that's a part of it, money is actually a lesser component. It's the preparation beforehand that will ultimately be of greater value to you. To the extent that you can acquire early knowledge and wisdom about wealth creation, your ability to manage significant wealth will be better assured.

And better than book knowledge is experience. By sharing some of my journey with you, I challenge you to start exercising the disciplines described in this book immediately. In doing so, you will amass your own wealth, and the money part of your inheritance will be the icing on the cake. As discussed later, you'll find that with God's help, achieving "self-made" status will be far more rewarding than inheriting wealth.

By the way, you are already rich. Really! When you consider mankind's history and the lifestyles of people in the world today compared to yours, you are already likely to be in the top 1–2% in terms of resources and opportunity. Specifically, people today with annual household incomes in excess of $32,500 are in the top 1% of the world's wealthiest families. I'm so thankful to my grandparents for the sacrifices they made along their journey to the United States so many years ago. They gave us the gift of opportunity.

To Fellow Parents and Grandparents

I suspect that many people today do not have the heritage of love and wisdom with which I and my family have been blessed. For those families who have yet to experience unconditional love, you're not unusual. I must admit, I took it for granted. I was cherished. One of the last visuals I have of my dad is him on his hospital bed as I was leaving. He was watching me go with a look of pride and love. That memory will accompany me to my last days.

To demonstrate unconditional love for our children and our grandchildren, we need to establish a legacy of loving wisdom. If we didn't receive it from our parents or grandparents, we can start it now—and we must.

—**Randall Sanada**

P.S. A Note about the Workbook

You'll notice that a workbook section, including reflective questions, application-oriented "action steps," and pages for notes, follows each main chapter of this book. These questions and practical steps are intended to help you think more deeply about biblical principles of financial stewardship and their relevance to your life. The workbook sections may prove useful for independent reflection, group study, or simply discussion with a friend or family member.

May this book prove a blessing to you, your children, and your grandchildren.

CHAPTER ONE

Wisdom Principles

*You shall teach them to your children ...
when you are walking by the way...*
– Deuteronomy 11:19 (ESV)

Why Wisdom First

How I wish I had spent more time with my grandparents. They came to the United States to pursue a better life for their family, and now we are living the dream they had for us. If only I had taken the time to write down everything they shared with me. I remember the days when Grandpa took me on walks in the desert, where he lived. He would share bits of wisdom from time to time. I remember one in particular: "Randall, listen to me now. You can accumulate a million dollars, but if you lose your health, you have nothing!" As he repeated this statement in his strong Italian accent, I knew that he spoke from experience. He had to move to the desert from Los Angeles because of his emphysema. He needed clean air to breathe.

I wonder if, during his later years, Grandpa wished he had taken more time with me and my siblings. Now at the age of 65, I certainly wish that I had spent more time with my sons, grandchildren, nephews, and nieces. As I write this, I am resolving to do just that. After all, I'm still alive and in good health, watching my diet and exercising almost every day. (Grandpa, your words didn't fall on deaf ears.) But the number of my days are fewer now, and I don't want to risk failing to impart those bits of wisdom that I feel need to be shared. Hence the writing of this book.

Sudden Wealth

Jack was incredulous. "$315 million!" He had just won the Powerball lottery! It was a time for joy and great celebration. Or was it? Jack's life changed dramatically, and sadly not for the better. Not long afterward, Jack was at a bar when someone broke into his car and stole a briefcase that had over a half-million dollars in it. His office and home were broken into, and he was twice arrested for drunk driving. His granddaughter died under suspicious circumstances, and within five years he had spent almost all of his money. He told reporters, "I wish I'd torn that ticket up."[1]

Jack Whittaker's lottery story from West Virginia has been widely reported in the media. Unfortunately, Jack's sad story is one of many.

Perhaps you've heard of other lottery winners who are less happy than they were before they won. Why is this? Would their stories have been different if they had been better prepared to manage their good fortunes?

The Inheritance

After his father's passing, Alex, age 28, was told by his dad's lawyer of the fortune he would inherit. He and his dad had never had a conversation about money. "Not a problem," Alex thought. "With an inheritance of over $1 million, it won't be difficult to figure out what to do." Alex had only fantasized about that one-ton Ford truck with the extended cab and diesel engine. Now he could buy it with all the upgrades. And he even put extra money down instead of going with the maximum financing.

After a few months of trying to decipher the investment statements from his dad's financial portfolio, Alex still couldn't really make sense of most of it. One thing was clear though: The portfolio was losing value. He had instructed his dad's financial advisor to distribute $10,000 per month from the portfolio so that Alex could enjoy income from his new wealth. After all, he figured he "deserved" an upgraded lifestyle, and he needed the money to make the payments on his new truck and the other purchases he had financed.

The advisor tried to counsel Alex not to take such a large draw from the portfolio, but Alex surmised that the portfolio was declining even faster than $10,000 per month. Alex wondered if this financial advisor wasn't doing his job very well, and he told him so. The advisor tried to explain the nature of the financial markets (where the portfolio was invested) and that they are prone to fluctuation. He encouraged Alex to be patient and to consider easing up on the lifestyle and withdrawal rate so that perhaps some opportunities could be pursued during the down market.

Meanwhile, Alex's cousin was starting a new business. He only needed $750,000 to get it going. He assured Alex that the business would easily be able to support a $10,000 per month distribution and that there would even be more to come.

Well, you can probably imagine the rest of the story. Alex told his dad's advisor that he had lost patience with him and that he had a better place to invest the money. And so, despite the advisor's warning—"Don't put all your eggs in one basket!"—Alex placed almost everything into his cousin's new business. But the cousin hadn't fully considered all the obstacles of starting and running a business, and it wasn't long before more capital was needed to keep the doors open. Alex didn't have any other money available to invest, and they were unable to find anyone else willing to help. The business closed, and the distributions stopped. The cousin was sincerely apologetic.

Alex was then left with very little of his inheritance, certainly not enough to supplement his employment income to a level where he could comfortably make the payments on his earlier purchases. Not many months later, the last of the inheritance was gone, and now Alex struggled to make all those payments. He found himself contemplating which items to give up. It looked like the truck would have to go. Depressed and ashamed, Alex was amazed at how quickly it all came and went. One thing was for sure: He wished he had been better prepared to handle his inheritance.

It turns out there's a lot of truth to the old saying, "From shirtsleeve to shirtsleeve in three generations." Indeed, 70% of the time, family fortunes are lost within a generation, and that number climbs to 90% within two generations.[2]

The father didn't err in leaving a good inheritance to his son. His failure was in not having imparted wisdom before the passing of wealth. In many ways, sudden wealth, whether in the form of an inheritance or other means, can be a curse instead of a blessing. I wonder if Alex ultimately wished his dad had left the money to someone else. His sad story is only one of many.

I know of another heir who was approached by a group promising to double his money in 90 days. His parents' advisors warned him that it was too good to be true. So he tested the group by investing $25,000. In 90 days instead of doubling his money, the group gave back $75,000. So he invested all of his liquid inherited funds with the group who then lost it all. This is why advisors warn their clients that they aren't leaving wealth to their unprepared heirs; but rather to the con artists.

Grandchildren, it's my hope that you will receive a good inheritance. It's also my hope to give you resources that will help you build wealth on your own. Then, you will also be equipped to handle any inheritance or other windfall that may come your way.

The Dangers of Inheritance

There are other dangers associated with receiving money without proper education about the principles of wealth management, according to Brad Klontz, a psychologist and Certified Financial Planner™. "The first generation to create the wealth normally did so coming from poverty or middle-class backgrounds. They had to work hard, and they made mistakes that they learned from. Along their paths to wealth, they became self-disciplined, resourceful and resilient." Klontz goes on to say, "You assume that those values will trickle down automatically, but your children are having a vastly different experience of the world than you had."[3] I know personally that as parents, we want to give our children the things we never had. We want to give them the best education and the latest toys; we want to pass on our wealth to them.

Warren Buffett once described the ideal inheritance for kids as "enough money so that they would feel they could do anything, but not so much that they could do nothing."[4] The inheritance left to children should follow a lifetime of imparting wisdom to them to protect it, grow it, and ultimately use it in a meaningful way.

> *Train up a child in the way he should go; even when he is old he will not depart from it.* — **Proverbs 22:6 (ESV)**

My parents and grandparents left small financial inheritances to my siblings and me, which we of course appreciated. But far more precious was the wisdom they imparted beforehand.

The Choice

Imagine that you're visiting a foreign land and you're exploring a cave. You sense that you may be one of the first people ever to be in this place. Then you discover a strange-looking lamp, and as you rub it to get a better look at it, out comes a genie. The genie declares that you are granted one wish. You think you're pretty smart and wish for three more wishes. "No-go" says the genie. "One wish only, what's it going to be?" Now think about this for a moment: Would you wish for riches, or would you wish to be granted wisdom?

Consider now these excerpts from a Biblical account:

> *"Give your servant therefore an understanding mind to govern your people, that I may discern between good and evil, for who is able to govern this your great people?" It pleased the Lord that Solomon had asked this. And God said to him, "Because you have asked this, and have not asked for yourself long life or riches or the life of your enemies, but have asked for yourself understanding to discern what is right, behold, I now do according to your word. Behold, I give you a wise and discerning mind, so that none like you has been before you and none like you shall arise after you. I give you also what you have not asked, both riches and honor, so that no other king shall compare with you, all your days.*
> *— 1 Kings 3:9–13 (ESV)*

One might surmise that Solomon was wise already to have made such a remarkable request. Regardless of how young you might be at this moment, as you think back on your life thus far, choices will doubtlessly come to mind that you have come to regret. Had you possessed greater wisdom at the time, better choices might have been made. Suffice it to say, as you go through life, the pursuit of wisdom will be a more than worthwhile endeavor. To best comprehend the value of wisdom, you must first develop an understanding of its nature and attributes.

What Is Wisdom?

Knowledge might be one of the first things that comes to mind when you contemplate the attributes of wisdom. The Greek word for 'knowledge' is gnosis, which indicates a straightforward grasp of facts, information, or doctrine gained through experience or education.

And while yes, it is an important part of wisdom, knowledge in itself does not equate to wisdom. Of course, you should accumulate knowledge while you're in school and in your professional studies to better equip you for life. But being able to rattle off facts from memory does not mean that you possess wisdom and understanding.

By contrast, sunesis is the Greek work for understanding and discernment. It literally describes "a running together, a flowing together [as] of two rivers."[5] In a sense, sunesis means that different strands of gnosis knowledge are flowing together into a deeper, wider comprehension.

Intelligence (Greek: Sunetos) is another attribute of wisdom, but again is insufficient in and of itself. Most people assume that genetics determine our level of intelligence. Actually that assumption is only about half correct.

A large body of research has shown that IQ is about 50% heritable.[6][7] This means that about half of the IQ variance among people is a result of genetic influences, but also that the other half of that variance is a result of environmental influences.[8]

So, intelligence can be developed and increased. But having a high IQ does not guarantee that you will be wise. After all, anyone can be tested to determine how smart or intelligent they are — which would give us an indication of the amount of knowledge they've acquired. But is there a measure or test to find out how wise someone is? Not exactly. Rather, we discern that wisdom exists in a person by observing the attributes they possess.

The Greek word for wisdom is sophia, which suggests the possession of skill[9]—that is, practical or applied knowledge (gnosis), intelligence (sunetos) and understanding (sunesis). Perhaps another way to say it is that wisdom comes from the mastery of applied knowledge, intelligence and understanding.

So then, how does one recognize wisdom? Perhaps the following list of attributes will help:

- Insight
- Prudence
- Discerning
- Discretion
- Learning
- Guidance
- Counsel
- Masterful understanding
- Competence
- Resourcefulness
- Expertise and skill

These virtues, as further described in the book of Proverbs, equip one to rule and give one the gravitas (or dignity) associated with wealth. Moreover, these capacities are exercised in the realms of righteousness, justice and equity, giving wisdom a moral dimension[10]

Wisdom is the ability to use intelligence and knowledge to think and act in such a way that common sense prevails. You can increase your intelligence from pouring over textbooks for hours, but you cannot acquire wisdom the same way. You cannot get enough knowledge to make you wise. You don't receive understanding from simply hearing or seeing information. Experience might be one of the most valuable tools for acquiring wisdom, other than acquiring the gift directly from God as King Solomon did.

You can hear lectures on swimming, you can read books on swimming, and you can understand the buoyancy of water from observation, but until you get into the water and get some experience, you won't have true wisdom about the water, and that may make all the difference between swimming and drowning. Experience is often the best teacher.

Acquiring Wisdom

There are multiple ways to acquire or grow in wisdom. Consider the following principles for personal wisdom development as well as recognizing the presence of wisdom in others.

Be afraid. Wisdom begins with the fear of the Lord. It isn't a fear of being struck dead by lightning, but a deep, abiding, holy reverence and respect for the Lord and for His Word, the Bible. The book of Proverbs has more to say about wisdom than any of the other books in the Bible. For example, Solomon said in

Proverbs, "The fear of the LORD is the beginning of wisdom, and the knowledge of the Holy One is insight" (Proverbs 9:10 ESV). I urge you to study the book of Proverbs as you seek God's wisdom in your life.

Obey and ask. From Proverbs and the rest of the Old Testament, we learn that sometimes obedience comes before understanding. When someone obeys what they know to be true, understanding usually follows.

But, what does the New Testament add to our understanding of wisdom? The book of James has been called the New Testament book of wisdom. It contains wisdom for the church and is considered part of the "wisdom literature." In this book James wrote, "If any of you lacks wisdom, let him ask God, who gives generously to all without reproach, and it will be given him" (James 1:5 ESV).

Now let's consider the following verse: "But let him ask in faith, with no doubting, for the one who doubts is like a wave of the sea that is driven and tossed by the wind" (James 1:6 ESV).

So it is appropriate for us to ask for and expect to receive wisdom. I've come to the realization that any hope of becoming a wise person in my own right is fruitless. Instead, my hope and prayer is to access God's wisdom and strength in my endeavors. I pray for this every day, especially as I prepare for important meetings and phone conversations.

Be disciplined. Throughout this text, there is considerable reference to the term "discipline." Unfortunately, discipline is typically perceived as a bad thing—as punishment. Most people do not like to be disciplined, but it is an important part of the learning process. "The rod and reproof give wisdom, but a child left to himself brings shame to his mother" (Proverbs 29:15 ESV). We know that children seek limits, and they crave understanding.

Discipline is orderly, rule-based behavior. Merriam-Webster defines 'discipline' as "a way of behaving that shows a willingness to obey rules or orders," "behavior that is judged by how well it follows a set of rules or orders," or "control that is gained by requiring that rules or orders be obeyed and punishing bad behavior."[11]

There is another aspect to discipline however, that can be most gratifying. I'm talking about self-discipline, which is "the ability to make yourself do things that should be done" or "correction or regulation of oneself for the sake of improvement."[12]

Please know that in most cases when I mention the word "discipline" in this text, I am referring to a form of self-discipline.

By the way, an excellent method for developing self-discipline is to establish proper priorities. Think about that for a moment: What are your life priorities? Mine are **faith, health, family,** and then **wealth.**

On any given day, it would be all too easy to neglect one or more of these priorities, especially the first two. But because of their extreme importance, I don't want to take any chances. So I start my day with a quiet time of prayer and reading Scripture. This provides spiritual nourishment and strength. Immediately afterward, I exercise and eat a healthy breakfast to strengthen and nourish the body. Having completed these two important items first thing in the morning, I'm then ready to address whatever else the day may bring. What gets done first, gets done.

And so self-discipline is another attribute that is likely to be found in a person of wisdom.

Keep wise counsel. Developing wisdom can take many years. One way to speed up the process is to spend time with wise people whenever possible.

But how do we identify those who can offer wise counsel? Let's explore a few attributes of people who typically possess wisdom.

Bear good fruit. Should we examine the life of those from whom we seek counsel? Consider their accomplishments, their failures, but also their life in general.

A good tree produces good fruit, and a bad tree produces bad fruit
—Matthew 7:17 (NLT)

So, what are the attributes that reflect the fruits of godly wisdom?

But the wisdom from above is first pure, then peaceable, gentle, open to reason, full of mercy and good fruits, impartial and sincere. —James 3:17 (ESV)

Learn from mistakes. Don't expect a wise person to be failure free. We often learn more from our failures than our successes, "for the righteous falls seven times and rises again, but the wicked stumble in times of calamity." (Proverbs 24:16 ESV). I know in my case, many of my mistakes have been valuable learning experiences. Bill, a friend of mine, recently quipped about a bumper sticker that he saw: "Oh no, not another learning experience!"

Pursue excellence. (not perfection). Perfectionists strive for impossible goals, but pursuers of excellence enjoy meeting high standards that are within reach. In the words of Confucius, "Better a diamond with a flaw than a pebble without."

Embrace the wisdom of experience. It helps if a person's been around for a while. Over the years, experience is amassed and wisdom can develop. Does this mean that wisdom will elude you until your later years? Consider the following scriptures:

> *I have more insight than all my teachers, for I meditate on your statutes. I understand more than the elders, for I obey your precepts.*
> **—Psalm 119:99–100 (NIV)**

And so, while age and experience are important, the sooner we learn and honor God's timeless precepts the sooner we are endowed with his wisdom.

Earned credentials. When seeking a person of wisdom, consider their academic achievements. If college degrees and certifications are not among their credentials, you'll want to consider why. Wise people likely have the discipline to complete various courses of study during their lifetimes. They also are likely to be involved in some kind of continued education.

This leads us to the matter of seeking wise counsel about your finances.

Financial Advisors

In the chapters that follow, I share a wide range of principles and techniques to help equip the reader with important elements of financial wisdom. For the students among you, these progressive building blocks will provide a primer that you can learn to use and practice yourself. But for all of you, be assured that there are many wise counselors to help you navigate this. Here's how to find the help you may seek.

What is the profile of a wise financial advisor? It helps if the advisor is of sufficient age to have gained significant professional experience. Consider their accomplishments. Are they a person of wealth, or do they lack discipline and live on credit? Has their counsel generated benefits for others? Of course, this doesn't mean that everything they touch must turn into gold.

An obvious prerequisite is that the financial professional possess one or more certifications. There are a number of credentialing programs that can equip a financial advisor with education beyond a college degree. I'll touch on just a couple of the most important:

CFP—Certified Financial Planner™. The CFP® designation is a professional certification conferred by the

Financial Planning Standards Board (FPSB) in the United States and 25 other territories around the world. There are now 160,000 CFP professionals worldwide. To receive authorization to use this designation, the candidate must meet education, examination, experience, and ethics requirements, and pay an ongoing certification fee. Subjects covered in the CFP exam are:

- General principles of finance and financial planning
- Insurance planning
- Employee benefits planning
- Investment and securities planning
- State and federal income tax planning
- Estate tax, gift tax, and transfer tax planning
- Asset protection planning
- Retirement planning

CKA® —Certified Kingdom Advisor.®[13] The CKA® designation identifies a class of accomplished financial professionals trained beyond standard industry credentials. The CKA® professional has undergone additional university-level training, passed a rigorous exam, and met other professional and ethical criteria. Equipped with biblically wise financial principles, the CKA® professional embraces a biblical worldview and thus enables their clients to navigate financial decisions as a faithful steward.

Certified Kingdom Advisor® is a designation granted by Kingdom Advisors to individuals who have demonstrated themselves as meeting certain standards:

Able to apply biblical wisdom in counsel. This is attained by participating in the Certified Kingdom Advisor® coursework and examination, and by a commitment to incorporating biblical principles in their financial advice.

Technically competent. This standard requires evidence of an approved professional designation (CFP,® ChFC,® CPA, CPA/PFS, EA, CFA, CIMA,® AAMS, CLU,® JD) or having at least 10 years of full-time experience in their discipline.

Ethical. This criterion is met by agreeing to espouse and practice the Kingdom Advisors Code of Ethics by maintaining active local church involvement and providing pastoral and client letters of reference.

Accountable. This standard indicates that they have agreed to submit themselves to annual accountability by another Certified Kingdom Advisor.®

Biblical stewards. The Certified Kingdom Advisor® pledges to practice biblical stewardship in their personal and professional lives, and to give regularly in proportion to their income.

The History of Kingdom Advisors

I was fortunate to be one of the founding members of Kingdom Advisors. We were a small group of sixteen, selected by Larry Burkett to be trained and equipped through scripture with financial principles and wisdom. We were to then be used by his ministry to provide pastors with a resource for those seeking biblically wise financial counsel. As Larry's health declined, we asked Ron Blue to take over the training responsibilities and then ultimately to become our president. Under Ron's leadership, the organization has grown to over 2,000 members, 1,000 of whom have earned certification.

The very first Kingdom Advisor actually dates back much further: Joe was naturally gifted with great wisdom and an ability to manage wealth, even though he came from a dysfunctional family. His first client ultimately placed his entire estate under Joe's management. And the estate prospered greatly. But the client's wife accused Joe of attempted rape (when in fact he refused her repeated advances), and Joe lost that client relationship—and ended up serving time in jail.

Ultimately, Joe was released and given a new opportunity to serve an even greater client: none other than the king himself. Here again, he excelled and brought greater wealth to his client, and at the same time predicted and prepared the country for a great depression. By the time the depression arrived, ample reserves were in place under Joe's leadership and a disaster was averted.

No doubt by now you realize that I am paraphrasing the story of Joseph, found in the book of Genesis (chapters 37–41). This account is the first story of a successful Kingdom Advisor. It is also an incredible story of perseverance and an example of God's providence.

Compass and Crown—Stewardship 101

Although seeking wisdom from a good financial advisor is important, nothing takes the place of pursuing your own education and experience.

A nine-week Bible study created by Howard Dayton that provides the most basic principles of stewardship is available at most churches. I like to refer to this course of study as "Stewardship 101." Two organizations, both founded by Howard Dayton, provide the materials for this study: Compass and Crown.

I highly recommend that every young person complete this course at their earliest possible opportunity—and then take it again as newlyweds. For those more advanced in age, the course can be beneficial to you as well, providing useful tools for you in your counsel to others.

The course addresses important principles such as the true ownership of wealth, avoidance of debt and cosigning, the pursuit of wise counsel, honesty, giving, work ethic, investing, training up children, contentment, and the impact of our finances on our eternity.

The course includes the following Money Map:[14]

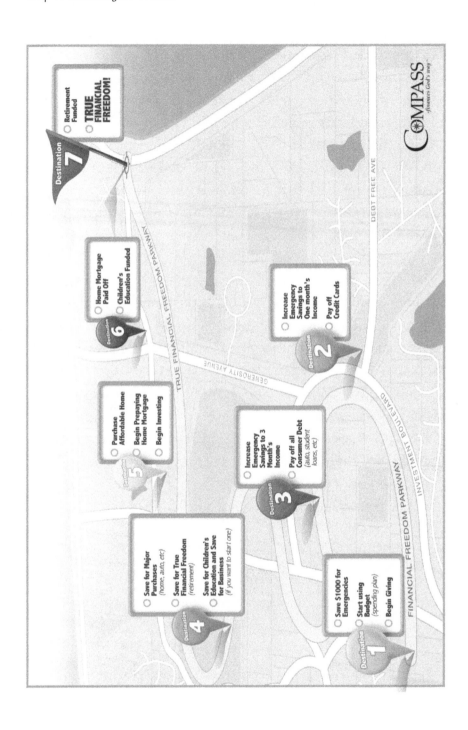

This map is used to gauge your progress during your financial journey. As you can see, the first steps involve the accumulation of reserves and the elimination of consumer debt. After that, you will be ready to begin your investment pursuits as described in the following chapters of this book.

Special Edition

There is a special edition of the Compass course designed for people who already possess wealth and who are addressing the associated challenges of a great many more alternatives and decisions. It's entitled "Charting Your Legacy," and is completed over the course of six weeks.

I have participated in the above courses and have found them life-changing—and humbling. When first introduced to the idea of signing up for the study, I couldn't see the point. First, I was too busy. Second, I reasoned, "What am I going to learn from this? As a credentialed financial advisor and a Christian who already tithes, I probably know all this stuff."

But then Larry Burkett and Howard Dayton addressed us during a Kingdom Advisors' conference to announce the merger of their organizations—Christian Financial Concepts and Crown. I figured it was time to complete the study, even though I didn't believe I needed it, just as a gesture of support. "Anyway," I thought, "my wife, Kay, can probably use this. She really has a problem with being too generous."

So we took the course together and sure enough, there was a major heart change—in me. I was the one who needed to learn about the joy of generosity, contentment, and a genuine comprehension of God's ownership versus my stewardship.

Before the study I actually believed that "contentment" was a bad word! As a Kingdom Advisor, I had been learning advanced principles of stewardship without having first completed the prerequisite: Compass/Crown—Stewardship 101. But now it all came together, and what I learned as a Kingdom Advisor took on greater meaning. Now my heart as well as my mind was prepared to receive the wisdom of genuine stewardship.

A final word about scriptural wisdom: it's timeless. As Judy Blue, wife of Ron Blue, has observed, "If it's true, it isn't new; if it's new, it isn't true."

There's so much more to learn about the pursuit of wisdom, and I urge you to devote a considerable amount of your energy to doing so.

But I expect that right about now, some of you are ready to remind me of Ecclesiastes 7:11 (ESV): "Wisdom is good with an inheritance…" So let's continue on with specific financial principles and strategies that will lead to your financial independence.

WORKBOOK

CHAPTER 1 QUESTIONS

Question: Why must wisdom come before wealth?

_____

_____

_____

_____

_____

_____

_____

_____

_____

Question: Which aspects of wisdom do you find the most challenging? How do your shortcomings in these areas affect your financial endeavors? What resources, measures, or daily habits could enable you to grow in these areas of wisdom?

_____

_____

_____

_____

_____

_____

_____

Question: Where do you find counsel, particularly on matters of investment and money management? How effective is your counsel? What are some good potential sources for wise counsel you might seek out?

_____

_____

_____

_____

_____

_____

_____

_____

Action: Put wisdom first, especially when it comes to money. Focus on acquiring not only knowledge, but also the wisdom to apply it with common sense. Practice habits that will develop specific aspects of wisdom in you. Seek out wise counsel and resources that will further your own education in biblical principles as well as in financial matters.

CHAPTER 1 NOTES

_____

_____

_____

_____

_____

_____

_____

_____

_____

_____

_____

_____

_____

_____

_____

_____

_____

_____

_____

_____

_____

_____

_____

_____

CHAPTER TWO

The Formula for Achieving Financial Independence

Have you ever had a great idea, and then found out you hadn't thought it through? Maybe you fantasized about achieving great wealth with it, but later realize the idea itself is ridiculous? I certainly have! If you'll bear with me, I'll share one of those ideas with you.

Dreams of Great Wealth—from a Penny

I was about four or five years old, sitting on my grandparents' front porch in downtown Los Angeles. The adults were talking about the value of a 1942D Lincoln Wheat penny, which was known to be rare and in demand. At the time, that special penny was worth about $50. The next thing I knew, they put me down for a nap and I couldn't sleep because I was too excited about how I was going to find one of those pennies and cash it in. "With that kind of money I'll be able to invest in what I covet most of all: toys! No wait, rather than spending the money right away, when I turn in the penny, I'll have them pay me in ... pennies!" I hadn't learned math yet, and didn't know how many pennies that would be, but I knew that it would be a lot. I thought certainly one of them would likely be another 1942D penny, which I would cash in for even more pennies. I was going to parlay that penny into thousands of dollars!

I thought that I had a plan for how I was going to achieve great wealth, all from that single penny. Not only would I have ample funds to buy toys, but I also wouldn't have to labor for money as an adult like my dad and my grandfathers.

Is it wrong or dumb to dream big dreams? Perhaps a dream is the beginning of a plan, which might result in an achievement. My young fantasy was obviously silly, but it was my first financial plan and the beginning of a concept in my mind: *it might be possible to find a way to achieve financial independence.*

Financial Independence Defined

Financial independence is the point at which your savings and investments generate enough income to equal or exceed your employment income. Or more specifically, the point at which they generate sufficient cash flow to cover the costs of your lifestyle. At this point, work becomes a choice and not a necessity. In this text, we will address the methodology of achieving financial independence.

In the past I jokingly said, "Financial independence is best achieved via the proper selection of one's parents." Now I jokingly say, "All I want for my children is that they have parents of immense wealth."

In reality, we know that inheriting wealth can be a mixed blessing—hence the need to acquire the wisdom and skills for independently achieving wealth first.

Is It Okay for Christians to Be Wealthy?

Some people get confused about this subject. They have read the book of 1 Timothy and have interpreted it as saying that money is sinful:

> *For the love of money is a root of all kinds of evils. It is through this craving that some have wandered away from the faith and pierced themselves with many pangs.* — **1 Timothy 6:10 (ESV)**

What does this verse mean to you? It seems to suggest that the sin lies in putting money ahead of God. With this in mind, consider the following scriptures on wealth and providence:

> *Thus says the Lord, your Redeemer, The Holy One of Israel: "I am the Lord your God, Who teaches you to profit, Who leads you by the way you should go.* — **Isaiah 48:17 (NKJV)**

> *And God will generously provide all you need. Then you will always have everything you need and plenty left over to share with others.* — **2 Corinthians 9:8 (NLT)**

> *With me are riches and honor, enduring wealth and prosperity.* — **Proverbs 8:18 (NIV)**

At the least, keeping an open mind on the subject is in order as we proceed first with a study of achieving financial independence and then financial freedom.

Compound Interest—Grandma's First Financial Lesson

I was a budding entrepreneur of about nine or ten years old when my grandmother noticed that I was accumulating a few dollars from mowing lawns and suggested that I open a savings account. I didn't see the point of it, so she explained to me that the money would be safer. She said the bank was a place that would keep the money from being misplaced or stolen. That made sense to me. Then she explained, "They also will pay you interest on the money that you deposit with them."

"Interest?" I asked, "Tell me more about this interest thing."

She said, "They will pay you 5% interest on the funds deposited with them. This means that they will give you a nickel each year for every dollar that you save with them. Then the next year they will give you 5% interest on your original dollar and 5% more on the nickel they gave you the first year."

At first I was a little skeptical. "Well, wait a minute. I thought they were doing the work of storing and protecting my money. Why would they pay me when they are the ones providing the service?" She briefly explained how they loaned my money out to other people at a higher interest rate and that a small portion of that could be paid to me.

What really captured my imagination was the fact that they would pay me interest on the money they had previously paid me. She said it was called "compound interest." I remember thinking that if I were to save enough money, the interest earnings could become significant. While a dollar would earn only a nickel, $100 would earn $5 and $1,000 would earn $50! And each year the account would grow even bigger because of compound interest. I imagined that eventually the account could grow so big from my deposits and the accompanying interest that it would generate enough income for me to live on. I wouldn't have to work another day in my life (at the time I was under the misconception that work was something to be dreaded).

I did open up a savings account, and the bank issued me a savings passbook.

Back then, the bank would give you a little book that would fit in your shirt pocket when you opened up your savings account. Every time my parents or grandparents brought me to the bank to make a deposit, the teller would write the deposit in my book. Once every three months, they would also record the interest that I had earned in my passbook.

At the time I didn't know it, but my parents were receiving my bank statements in the mail. All I had at the time was this humble savings passbook. Putting money in my account and seeing the interest earnings get bigger because of my investing was mesmerizing! (See the appendices 1 and 2 for a biblical perspective and detailed description of interest earnings and compound interest.)

Financial Independence on Interest Earnings

At the time my grandma taught me about compound interest, I was in the business of mowing lawns. I took pride in my work, and when neighbors would drive by and see me working, some would say, "Why don't you come mow my lawn?" I would bring my dad's push-mower down the street with the clippers in my back pocket and mow their lawns. I had a few calluses and an occasional blister, but my customers had the best-looking lawns in the neighborhood.

I was paid about 50 cents each time I mowed (believe it or not, a reasonable wage in those days). I saved most of what I earned, excited about the concept of compound interest. I dreamt of the day when the interest earnings on my savings would be as much or more than my lawn mowing earnings *—I had arrived at another little plan for achieving financial independence.*

But this time there were some viable aspects to it. The key ingredients for achieving financial independence were now becoming known to me:

- Savings amount
- Investment yield
- Time

So the math is simple: as you save and invest, the investment returns (interest earnings) will ultimately grow and compound to the point where they can be quite significant. Basically, the concept is to harness money so it is working for you and can someday relieve you of the necessity of employment. This can be the outcome of earning enough compound interest!

During my lawn-mowing days, I didn't quite know how to complete the math on achieving financial independence via my little plan. But here it is in retrospect:

- *Savings amount:* Suppose I mowed lawns 20 times per month at 50 cents each, thus earning $10 per month. Suppose that I saved 80% of that amount, thereby saving $8 per month.
- *Investment yield:* 5%
- *Time:* 16 ½ years

This means that by saving $8 per month in an account earning 5% interest, the account balance would grow to $2,400 in 16 ½ years. That $2,400, still earning 5% interest, would yield $120 per year, or $10 per month, thus matching my lawn mowing earnings.

Well, maybe not the most encouraging outcome. Sixteen and a half years is a long time for a kid. Passbook savings accounts don't always pay 5% (as I write this, their yield is less than 1%). And who has the ability to save 80% of their income, anyway? Small savings amounts and low investment yields produce low results. A better formula was needed. But the seeds were there for further development.

The Journey to Financial Independence—the Basics

I realize that the introduction of these compound interest principles is very basic and that many people reading this book already know this information. My purpose is to impart this material to my young grandchildren and other young people who have yet to be exposed to these principles. Interestingly, I've encountered many adults who have indicated that they didn't really have a full grasp on the effects of compound interest and were surprised to learn of its profound power to create wealth—it's been described as "the eighth wonder of the world," and not without reason. Therefore, it's worth taking the time to nail down these basics before progressing to more advanced concepts.

Double Teenage Net Worth Every Year

Just before starting college, my net worth had grown to a few thousand dollars. It occurred to me that if I worked and saved diligently, I could double that net worth in a year. In my naiveté, I extrapolated the idea of doubling again each year until I had achieved financial independence. Another crazy idea (just like the 1942D penny), but it encouraged me to become disciplined and to embrace planning. I was still better off financially even as I realized that I needed a more reasonable plan.

Rule of 72

Although my youthful idea of doubling my net worth every year was a bust, I did discover along the way the rule of how money doubles itself through compound interest.

The Rule of 72 provides the simple math in calculating how long it takes for money to double at a given interest rate. For example, if an investment produces a 6% interest rate, you merely need to divide 72 by 6 to know that it will take 12 years for the investment to double.

This rule also can be used to determine what an investment is yielding if you know how long it takes for it to double. Example: If an investment has doubled in 10 years, by dividing 10 into 72 you will know that the yield on that investment was 7.2%.

The Rule of 72 is a great tool when you are in need of a quick mental calculation on the doubling of money.

Enter the Computer

In college, I pursued a double major in Business Management and Data Processing (computers). When it came time to develop my first solo computer program, I was given the opportunity to determine the subject matter. You probably won't be surprised to learn that I chose to write a program to calculate the long-term effects of compound interest. I figured such a program could be a valuable tool. Once it was finished, I soon found a situation where this tool could be put to use.

A friend of a friend had recently sold me a whole life insurance policy on the basis that it would be a good investment. If I paid into the policy every month, cash values would eventually begin accumulating, and in the long term they would amount to a large sum of money. In those days, banks were still paying 5% interest, and I wondered how much would accumulate there if I deposited the same amount as I was paying to the insurance company. I entered the data and ran the program—and the results were surprising. A low-interest bank account would grow to a dramatically larger sum than would the insurance policy. It turns out insurance, while valuable as a risk mitigation tool, was not a worthwhile investment.

I used this program to show fellow students and friends how they could benefit from compound interest, and soon found myself somewhat in demand as a money and budgeting counselor. I sure enjoyed doing that, and I dreamt of the day that I might become a financial advisor of some sort.

It wasn't long afterward when the opportunity literally walked in the door. Kay and I married just after my junior year in college, and one afternoon I was helping her carry the laundry downstairs from our apartment. Shortly after we arrived in the laundry room, a nicely dressed gentleman entered and asked for directions to one of the apartments.

I chose to walk him over, and while doing so I asked if he was an insurance salesman. He cleared his throat, somewhat offended, and stated that he was a financial advisor. "Interesting," I said, "I'm going to be a financial advisor someday myself." Next thing I knew, the district manager from IDS had me on the phone, suggesting that I should interview with them. I asked if they would have any objection to my intentions of working part-time for a number of companies so I could address securities investments, real estate, insurance, banking, etc.

"No," he said, "you'll be required to work full time for us."

"Too bad," I said. "I feel that it's important to be diversified in order to fully address all my future clients' needs."

He replied, "Diversified—why, that's our middle name! IDS stands for Investors *Diversified* Services." Not long afterward, I was accepted as a full-time trainee, having (barely) convinced them that I could do so while completing my degrees during my senior year of college.

My computer skills were soon put to work in my young professional career. My senior project in college needed to cover both of my degrees, business and computers. I decided to write a program that would produce a financial plan. The software would learn from previous runs and would then upgrade the computer's recommendations over time. I thought I was creating (what is now called) artificial intelligence, but in fact it was nowhere near that sophisticated.

The learning algorithm was more difficult than I had contemplated, and time was running out as the due date approached. One night I awoke with the solution, wrote it down on a pad, put it on my nightstand, and went back to sleep. The next morning, I looked at what was likely to be another lame idea, but this one was sound (perhaps because it had nothing to do with a 1942D penny). The software was a success, and I got an A. My clients liked it too, and during my first year at the firm, I was the top-producing advisor in my division.

Before long, I received a call from IDS headquarters. The idea of a computer-assisted financial plan was something they had been thinking about, and they wanted to buy my software. Later, IDS became a subsidiary of American Express, which was added to their name.

My career at IDS American Express (now called Ameriprise) ultimately proved short. After fifteen years with them, my investment portfolio was producing enough income to support our lifestyle, so I retired. I had achieved my young dreams of financial independence. I had harnessed money so that it was working for me, not the other way around.

That reminds me—during my time at IDS American Express, they briefly aired a TV commercial about money. It depicted a large, greedy man who was laughing as he sat at his huge banquet table. Then he introduced himself: "Do you know me? I am Money. Sure, you know me. You work for me. And why am I laughing? *Because I should be working for you!*" The commercial didn't air for long. Apparently, it wasn't very well received. But I got the point completely. Why would anyone want to spend their life working for money when it should be the other way around? And for that matter, in a society such as ours, the most materially prosperous in the history of mankind, everyone should be financially independent, or should at least have a plan to achieve that status.

Is It Appropriate to Be Retired?

I was retired and living the good life—or so I thought. One Tuesday morning, while sitting in the Jacuzzi with Kay, I asked if she agreed how wonderful it was to be able to do this all the time. "Honestly?" she said. "We have four young children and a big house to manage, and frankly you're getting under foot."

Actually, I was relieved to hear this, because sitting in the Jacuzzi almost every day was getting boring. So I opened an office around the corner to manage our investment holdings. I hired an assistant, Keith, to help with administration so I could focus on finding more good investment opportunities and expanding our holdings. Friends and former clients expressed an interest in investing alongside our family, as I hoped they would. Together we could pursue the acquisition of larger investment opportunities and achieve better diversification. And so our single-family office became a multi-family office.

We named our new enterprise Alliance. We hired more staff and financial professionals, bought a broker dealer, and ultimately formed a bank and trust company in partnership with some other financial services firms. Today, our two oldest sons, Randy Jr. and Jerry, run the enterprise, which encompasses twenty-two companies.

I'm still involved, but also spend time in ministry pursuits, serving alongside organizations like Kingdom Advisors, Compass, Kingdom Centers, and Christian Foundation of the West. I tried and failed at the idea of retirement. It turns out there's no mention of retirement in the Bible, other than for priests. While times of leisure are nice, boredom can quickly set in. God made us in His image and instructed us to dominate the earth, working and creating with meaningful purpose.

Rather than retirement, I've found "rewirement" to be the better model for me. Pursuing new and exciting opportunities while serving in ministries that bless others is what I feel God has in mind for me. And yes, He seems to be okay with my also having other types of fun like hitting the ski slopes, flying planes, and driving race cars with my sons and grandchildren.

Financial Independence—Formula 15

You know my story on achieving financial independence. Now it's time to discuss a way for you to do it too. Recall the definition of financial independence: It is the point where your investment income is sufficient to meet your lifestyle cash-flow needs. At this point, work is a choice rather than a necessity. In a society such as ours, everyone should at least have a plan of financial independence, if not already achieved.

Think for a moment about your favorite cake. Perhaps your mom or your grandmother made it for you. You know that in order for that cake to be delicious, she had to follow a certain recipe. And within that recipe were the key ingredients. The three ingredients that make up the formula for financial independence are:

- Savings amount
- Investment return
- Time

Basically, if you save a given percentage of your income and can earn a given yield on your savings and investments, you will amass an investment portfolio large enough to produce income to meet your lifestyle within a determinable number of years. Naturally, the more you save and the higher your investments yield, the sooner you will achieve financial independence. Thus unlike a cake recipe, the ingredients can be variable. There can be many different formulas that will achieve the intended results, but the following one is probably the easiest to understand and remember. Formula 15 simply stated is

> Save/invest 15% of your income
> Earn a yield of 15% on these savings/ investments
> You will be financially independent in 15 years.

Right about now, you may be thinking that this concept is another 1942D penny fantasy. It's not. We must be careful though not to set unrealistic expectations, like averaging investment returns of 15%. Bear with me for a bit and we'll get to that and a number of other challenges.

The formula works at any level of income. For example, if you earn $80,000 per year, and save 15% of that amount, you are investing $12,000 per year towards your financial independence. If you average a 15% rate of return on your investments, in 15 years you will accumulate over $570,000. If that $570,000 continues to generate a 15% yield, it will produce over $80,000 per year in earnings from which you can support your lifestyle.

Here's the schedule:

Annual Income			$	80,000.00
Annual Savings %				15%
Annual Savings $			$	12,000.00

Year	Investment	Interest @ 15%	Balance
1	$ 12,000	--	$ 12,000
2	$ 12,000	$ 1,800	$ 25,800
3	$ 12,000	$ 3,870	$ 41,670
4	$ 12,000	$ 6,251	$ 59,921
5	$ 12,000	$ 8,988	$ 80,909
6	$ 12,000	$ 12,136	$ 105,045
7	$ 12,000	$ 15,757	$ 132,802
8	$ 12,000	$ 19,920	$ 164,722
9	$ 12,000	$ 24,708	$ 201,430
10	$ 12,000	$ 30,215	$ 243,645
11	$ 12,000	$ 36,547	$ 292,191
12	$ 12,000	$ 43,829	$ 348,020
13	$ 12,000	$ 52,203	$ 412,223
14	$ 12,000	$ 61,833	$ 486,056
15	$ 12,000	$ 72,908	$ 570,965

The formula can be modified by changing the savings amount and/or yield, which will result in a different outcome in terms of years to financial independence. The following matrix provides a sampling of additional formulas:

Financial Independence Formulas

Savings as a Percentage of Income	6%	9%	12%	15%	18%
30%	26	18	13	11	9
27%	27	18	14	12	10
24%	29	20	15	12	10
21%	31	21	16	13	11
18%	33	22	17	14	12
15%	35	24	18	15	13
12%	39	26	20	16	14
9%	43	29	23	18	16

Investment Yield

See appendix 3 ("Financial Independence Formulas") for an expanded matrix of the formulas. Achieving financial independence sounds easy enough, right? Not really. You are probably already thinking of the challenges. Let's discuss them:

Challenges to Formula 15

There are four main challenges to the successful execution of this formula. Remember them easily with the acronym "DIRT."

You probably expect the D to stand for debt. That's a part of it, but the word we're looking for here is *discipline*. We discuss discipline (or the lack thereof) throughout this text as the number one barrier to achieving financial independence. It's not easy to set aside 15% of your income and then leave it alone for 15 years. If you disturb your favorite cake before it rises, it can be ruined. So you have to be patient. Likewise, you need to allow your financial independence fund to rise to its goal before tasting of its benefits.

There are many demands on our cash flow, and the temptation to spend it all—and yes, even beyond (via the use of debt)—can be a challenge for all of us. Thus discipline is crucial, and it helps if we establish our priorities. We know that the government will get its share first (in the form of income taxes) before we ever see the net amount of our paychecks. Upon receipt of our net amount, one of our first priorities should be saving toward our financial independence. The principle here is to learn to pay yourself, immediately after paying taxes to the government and tithing to God. Prioritization is one of the most critical elements of our cash-flow strategy.

And of course, avoiding consumer debt is another important part of discipline. If you allow credit card interest to consume any amount of your income, your cash flow can be severely cramped. Think about it: just as the math of compound interest can work for you in amazing ways, so does it work the same for the credit card companies—but at your expense. Don't ever allow credit card companies to charge you interest! Never purchase anything with a credit card unless you know that you will be able to pay for it in full when the statement arrives at the end of the month.

The second challenge is *inflation*. We know that 15 years from now, $80,000 won't purchase what it does today. The primary way we overcome inflation is quite natural: If we save 15% of an ever-increasing salary, the amount invested each year will increase, hopefully in step with or ahead of inflation. This, along with enhanced investment returns, is what's required to offset the effects of inflation.

The third challenge is *risk*. In order to generate a 15% rate of return, to what kind of risk must we subject our investments? For that matter, are there investments that consistently produce a 15% yield? The stock market (S&P 500) has averaged 11.07% over the last 40 years, and bonds have produced only a 7.36% return over the same period (Barclays U.S. Agg)[15]. And these returns have not been without risk.

Candidly, there are few investments that have generated a 15% rate of return (for more than short periods of a time) without being leveraged. And consistently earning double-digit returns, even for leveraged investments, is a tall order. An example of leverage would be real estate investments in which the bank provides a significant portion of the working capital. We'll spend some time in the next chapter discussing leverage and investment strategies for enhanced returns and reduction of risk.

Regardless, your personal plan of financial independence should not assume a consistent 15% annual increase in your investments. Formula 15 is a hypothetical example of how the three components (savings amount, yield, and time) can converge for an easy to remember concept.

Something else to keep in mind; it is prudent to reduce the risk exposure as you get older and especially as you enter your retirement years. And often, with reduced risk comes reduced investment yields. Formula 15, and all the formulas on the matrix above, assume that the investment yields stay the same after retirement. If you lower the yield assumption for the years when you are drawing from the portfolio, a larger amount of capital will be required. For example if you decide to draw 4% from your portfolio (a standard practiced by many advisors), then in order to receive $80,000 in annual income you will need to have $2 million in your retirement portfolio. That's substantially more than the $570,965 accumulated in the earlier example.

Don't be discouraged by this. You'll find that as time goes by and you build your investment skills, accumulating a multimillion dollar investment portfolio isn't all that difficult. Keep in mind also that there are other sources to help supplement your retirement income goal such as Social Security, pensions, inheritances, etc.

You may be wondering why the draw rate is only 4%? Is that all one could hope to earn on their investments during retirement? No, a conservative portfolio will hopefully earn 6-7% or perhaps more. The reason for drawing only 4% is that you will want to allow some of the interest to accumulate and grow the principal so that larger amounts can be withdrawn over the years to adjust for inflation. The typical intent is to keep principal intact for life and then pass it to heirs and/or charity afterwards. In later years, a higher draw rate is acceptable, and even some invasion of principal.

It's not difficult to calculate the draw amount that will keep principal from running out until a specified age, such as age 100. For examples, see www.WisdomB4Wealth.com.

The final challenge is *taxes*, the T in D.I.R.T. We know that federal and state governments will demand a part of these earnings, and our compliance is to be expected:

Pay to all what is owed to them: taxes to whom taxes are owed...
—Romans 13:7 (ESV)

Fortunately, the tax laws offer a number of methods by which to defer taxes and even enjoy tax-exempt earnings. Check with your advisor about the use of 401(k)s, IRAs, 457 plans, 403(b)s, and other savings plans to *defer* taxes and earn compound interest for yourself on those deferred amounts. To *exempt* earnings from taxes, look into the Roth IRA and municipal bonds.

The above is only a brief overview of the challenges in Formula 15. For now, suffice it to say that they are formidable and require a considerable amount of thought and effort to overcome.

The purpose of this chapter is to whet your appetite for the possibility of achieving financial independence by utilizing one of many available formulas.

Seek wise, professional assistance, especially as your resources increase, and together you and your advisor can arrive at a plan that will enable you to optimize a customized version of the Formula 15 strategy that will put you on a path toward financial independence.

WORKBOOK

CHAPTER 2 QUESTIONS

Question: What are your financial dreams and goals?

_____

_____

_____

_____

_____

_____

_____

_____

_____

Question: Where are you on your personal journey to financial independence? What obstacles have you overcome, and which do you still face?

_____

_____

_____

_____

_____

_____

_____

_____

Question: How can you begin to use or adapt Formula 15 to work for your situation? How can your version of Formula 15 help you overcome your particular financial challenges? What specific next steps will you take?

_____

_____

_____

_____

_____

_____

_____

_____

Action: Don't dismiss the importance of dreams, even far-fetched ones, that can lead to something real. And be willing to dream big! Figure out a plan to make money work for you, knowing that you can still be productive even if you reach a point where you don't have to work for a living. Recognize the challenges you face, but know that it's possible with God, wise counsel, and discipline.

CHAPTER 2 NOTES

_____
_____
_____
_____
_____
_____
_____
_____
_____
_____
_____
_____
_____
_____
_____
_____
_____
_____
_____
_____
_____
_____
_____
_____
_____

CHAPTER THREE

Investing for Financial Independence

S peaking of whetting appetites, occasionally clients will arrive at our office accompanied by their young children. Realizing that the children will likely be bored by our conversation, I'll sometimes offer an interesting exercise to keep them occupied.

I'll ask them to consider a short-term job where the employer offers them a choice of compensation arrangements. Suppose you are offered either $1,000 a day for thirty days *or* one cent that's doubled every day for thirty days. I then give the young person a piece of paper and a pencil and encourage them to do the math.

Which offer would you take? Most people, when asked, will quickly select the $1,000 per day offer. Here are the outcomes of the two options:

• $1,000 per day times 30 days equals $30,000.

- One penny doubled every day for thirty days amounts to over $10,000,000. See the following chart for the math.

This is an extreme example of compounding. But it can spark the imagination of a young person as they begin to contemplate compounding's effects.

	Daily Amount	Cumulative Total
Day 1	$ 0.01	$ 0.01
Day 2	$ 0.02	$ 0.03
Day 3	$ 0.04	$ 0.07
Day 4	$ 0.08	$ 0.15
Day 5	$ 0.16	$ 0.31
Day 6	$ 0.32	$ 0.63
Day 7	$ 0.64	$ 1.27
Day 8	$ 1.28	$ 2.55
Day 9	$ 2.56	$ 5.11
Day 10	$ 5.12	$ 10.23
Day 11	$ 10.24	$ 20.47
Day 12	$ 20.48	$ 40.95
Day 13	$ 40.96	$ 81.91
Day 14	$ 81.92	$ 163.83
Day 15	$ 163.84	$ 327.67
Day 16	$ 327.68	$ 655.35
Day 17	$ 655.36	$ 1,310.71
Day 18	$ 1,310.72	$ 2,621.43
Day 19	$ 2,621.44	$ 5,242.87
Day 20	$ 5,242.88	$ 10,485.75
Day 21	$ 10,485.76	$ 20,971.51
Day 22	$ 20,971.52	$ 41,943.03
Day 23	$ 41,943.04	$ 83,886.07
Day 24	$ 83,886.08	$ 167,772.15
Day 25	$ 167,772.16	$ 335,544.31
Day 26	$ 335,544.32	$ 671,088.63
Day 27	$ 671,088.64	$ 1,342,177.27
Day 28	$ 1,342,177.28	$ 2,684,354.55
Day 29	$ 2,684,354.56	$ 5,368,709.11
Day 30	$ 5,368,709.12	$ 10,737,418.23
Total	$ 10,737,418.23	

Now let's dig into the serious and decidedly non-hypothetical topic of investing.

Investing

Investing versus Gambling

As we begin this chapter on investing, it's important to start with a clear understanding of the differences between investing and gambling. Most people know that gambling is foolish. For starters, the likelihood of loss is greater than the likelihood of gain. The gambling establishments (they now use the word "gaming") set the terms of the transaction so that they are favored to win, and you are likely to lose.

Gambling always produces losses over time. You may win occasionally or even frequently, but this only sets you up for even bigger losses. In order for someone to win in gambling, someone else has to lose—that someone is ultimately going to be you if you choose to participate. A good financial steward avoids gambling and its associated risks.

Unfortunately, some people look at the fact that investing also involves risk and therefore liken it to gambling. These people don't understand the fundamental difference between investing and gambling: Investing typically involves the creation of value. Instead of a win-lose scenario, investing should be win-win.

When you invest in a company that is selling a product or service, it provides value to its customer and makes a profit for you, typically paid to you in the form of dividends. Then when you sell your stock in the company, hopefully for an additional profit, the buyer of the stock intends to continue making profits going forward. Win-win. Granted, there is risk of loss if things go wrong. But the intention is to create value and make a profit.

Likewise, when you invest in rental property, the tenant pays rent for value received and you enjoy the income and tax write-offs, with the added hope of selling the property for a profit in the future. Win-win.

Investments create jobs, deliver value and create wealth. Obviously this is very different from gambling. Keep in mind, however, that not all "investment opportunities" offer rewards commensurate with their associated risk. Therefore, it is wise to seek the counsel of a qualified investment advisor.

In This Period of Uncertainty...

As we contemplate the following investment principles, we first need to recognize the nature of our investment environment. No doubt as you read this book today, you are mindful of the media's frequent mention of the fact that we are in a period of "uncertainty." Whenever I hear that statement, I ask myself: When have we ever been in a period of "certainty"? With over fifty years of investment experience (forty-five years as a professional), I cannot recall any moment when there was certainty of any kind within the investment realm.

Heraclitus, a philosopher who lived 500 years before Christ, said, "The only thing that is constant is change." Likewise, most of our investments are going to fluctuate in value, especially those traded in the financial markets, such as stocks and bonds. Most people assume that fluctuation is bad, especially when it is to the downside.

While fluctuation can be uncomfortable (nobody enjoys seeing their stock portfolio lose value), in reality this fluctuation can be harnessed to produce greater investment returns. We'll talk about how when we discuss the Asset Balance Matrix* and dollar cost averaging. We'll also discuss how to tame the uncomfortable effects of fluctuation as we explore the principle of diversification. But first, a brief overview of investment securities.

What Is a Bond?

A bond is a loan to a corporation or government. The loan amount is typically in increments of $1,000, and it is for a stated period of time at a specified interest rate. For example, a 30-year bond paying 5% will pay $50 per year in exchange for your $1,000 investment, and will then return your $1,000 at the end of that 30 years. Given the long-term nature of bonds, there is a public market that enables investors to buy and sell these bonds so that investors are not locked in for the full term of 30 years.

The market value of the bond moves inversely with interest rate fluctuations. Hence, if you purchase a long-term 5% bond today and then decide to sell it later, at a time when the market commands a higher interest rate, you will find that the market value of your bond is less than you paid. Hopefully though, you earned enough interest in the interim to offset that loss. On the other hand, if the market is satisfied with a lower interest rate at the time of your bond sale, you will receive a premium above your cost, on top of the interest earnings you already received, resulting in an enhanced investment return. The following is a simplified example:

Face Value	$1,000
Coupon Rate	5%
Annual Interest Earnings	$50

If the market demand changes to 6%:

$50 ÷ 6% = $833 market value (a $167 loss)

If you owned the bond for at least four years before selling, your total return would be calculated as follows:

$50 × 4 = $200 + $833 = $1033

A total gain of only $33 on your $1,000 investment is minimal, but at least you didn't lose money selling in a down market.

If, on the other hand, the market demand changes to only 4%:

$50 ÷ 4% = $1250 market value (a $250 gain)

Selling this bond after four years in this market would result in the following:

$50 × 4 = $200 + $1250 = $1450

Here you made a 45% return in just four years, which is far better than a simple 5% per year investment would suggest.

These are very simple calculations to demonstrate the impact of changing interest rates on your investment return using bonds. They don't take into consideration that these bonds will eventually mature at their $1,000 face amount, so these illustrated market fluctuations are thus exaggerated. To see more detailed calculations that determine "yield to maturity," visit www.WisdomB4Wealth.com.

You can make money in bonds—typically not a lot, but a reasonable amount given the low risk associated with them. However, you can also lose money in bonds, especially if you choose to sell them at a time when interest rates have gone up.

What Is a Stock?

One of the most common investments is stocks. Owning a share of stock represents ownership in a company, specifically a corporation. Theoretically, the total value of that company is represented by the number of stock shares outstanding multiplied by the current price of one share of that stock. If it is a public company, the shares are traded on a public exchange such as the New York Stock Exchange or the NASDAQ.

Given that these shares are traded on these exchanges every business day, there is natural fluctuation in their value, even if there have been no significant changes in the status of the corporation that day. Supply and demand, not necessarily the intrinsic value of the corporation, determines the price of a stock at any given moment. As a result, there may be opportunities to buy or sell when the market overreacts, as it typically does. Given that there are literally thousands of corporations whose shares are traded publicly, there are a lot of stocks to choose from—hence the demand for professional management.

What Is a Mutual Fund?

A mutual fund is a portfolio of professionally managed stocks and/or bonds. For a small management fee, the management firm provides daily oversight of the portfolio, selecting the securities (stocks and bonds) that they believe will deliver the greatest investment returns for a given level of risk. As such, the investor has the benefit of diversification and professional management to help optimize their investment returns. A mutual fund that diversifies across most of the different industries in this country can be considered an investment in American enterprise overall.

There are many variations on these mutual funds: corporate bonds, government bonds, municipal bonds, common stock, preferred stock, open end funds, closed end funds, exchange traded funds (ETFs), etc. It will be worth your while to learn about these in considerably more detail. See the website www.WisdomB4Wealth.com to gain greater insight and to find educational resources. In addition, you should seek counsel from an investment professional to help you determine what mix of these securities should be present in your investment portfolio.

In our earlier discussion of Formula 15, we observed a number of challenges, one of which was the challenge of finding good investment returns and then dealing with their associated risks. With this in mind, one might be somewhat discouraged about the idea of finding higher yielding investments. And while it's important to proceed with caution in this area, implementing the principles of diversification and balance can mitigate a significant amount of that risk.

Diversification—Preparing for the Best Worst-Case Scenario

Mark came to us shortly after the 1987 stock market crash. He was concerned about his inherited holdings in a telecom stock. It had done very well over the years, but had recently plunged along with the rest of the stock market. Although he still had confidence in the telecom company, he was unsure whether he could further stomach the extreme volatility of his net worth, because this stock represented the majority of his investment holdings.

My counsel was to diversify. Mark agreed and we proceeded to reallocate his portfolio into a blend of investments in accordance with an Asset Balance Matrix˙ (to be described shortly). Of course, he kept a healthy portion of the telecom stock as well, but now his fortunes were no longer exclusively tied to this one company.

Mark slept better, yet over time the telecom stock soared! Had he kept all of his money in just that stock, he would have been much better off. The remainder of his diversified portfolio did fine however, generating respectable returns, and he was financially secure. In fact, he was now a multi-millionaire. Mark lived out his days in comfort and security and had no regrets. Had the company failed while he had all his eggs in that basket, he would have lost almost everything. Instead, while he earned significant gains in the telecom company, his diversified portfolio allowed him peace of mind.

Around the same time, Dan came to me with a similar situation. He owned a substantial amount of a tech company's stock. He was a consultant for the company and felt that he knew it very well. Thus, when I advised him to diversify as Mark did, Dan rejected the idea and chose instead to keep almost all of his eggs in that one investment basket. Dan had set a goal for his stock to reach $10 million in value, and then he would consider my counsel to harvest some of his gains in order to diversify his holdings.

Then the worst thing happened to Dan: The tech company failed, and so did Dan. Having no other major assets but his house and a significant mortgage, Dan was forced to sell that property and move out of state in search of a lower cost of living. Today he lives the lifestyle afforded to him primarily by Social Security.

In both cases, the worst thing happened. One client flourished regardless; the other did not. My vote is and always will be for diversification and balance. Let's discuss this in detail.

Putting Your Eggs in Different Baskets

> *Give a portion to seven, or even to eight, for you know not what disaster may happen on earth.* — **Ecclesiastes 11:2 (ESV)**

In light of this scripture and the examples presented in the previous section, one of the first investment instructions I can give you is: *Don't put all of your eggs in one basket!* This basic concept—technically the term is "diversification"—is simple enough to comprehend. If you place all of your investment dollars into only one or two investments, you are subjecting yourself to high and unnecessary risk. Remember also the earlier story of Alex, who placed almost all of his inheritance into a new business venture with his cousin? He was very unwise. We know that most investments fluctuate; some do so on their way to failure. Because we don't know in advance which ones will succeed and which ones will fail, it is critical that we diversify our risks.

Let's pause for a moment and consider an important question: Why invest in fluctuating investments in the first place, given that there are many investments that don't fluctuate? The simple answer is yield. Yes, there are safe non-fluctuating investments, like insured bank savings accounts, CDs, and T-bills. And yes, investments like these have a place in your overall investment portfolio. But the simple fact is that you are trading yield for safety. The average long-term investment return on these safe investments is very low in comparison to those available in the financial markets (stocks, bonds, mutual funds) and in tangible investments such as real estate. These can produce significant, possibly even double-digit returns, but the safety factor is significantly affected.

Diversification means that we use many different types of investments within our portfolio to pursue higher returns while simultaneously softening the fluctuation with a proper blend of safe investments.

"The more diversified the better" is a statement I often made during media interviews when I briefly served as a spokesman for IDS American Express. Then my day of reckoning arrived. It was during a live television interview with a local financial reporter. We were responding to callers who were asking questions. I had been describing the benefits of diversification and explaining my reasoning when one caller made an observation rather than asking a question. "Randall, I generally agree with your remarks on diversification, but when you say 'the more the better,' I have to wonder if you've thought it through completely. It seems to me that if one diversifies equally across the full spectrum of investment opportunities, at best his overall returns will be average or mediocre."

"Uh … well, yes," I responded. You see, I had touted diversification as a panacea—as more than just the answer for risk mitigation. The simple fact is that if you are smart enough to predict accurately the one most profitable investment for the future, you'd actually be better off putting all your money into that one investment. In this situation, diversifying into other investments (that don't quite generate the same high profits) would only lower your overall portfolio return (like in Mark's story).

But the reality is that no one is capable of accurately predicting the future, especially when it comes to investment returns. Hence the need to diversify and also the need to understand that with the reduction of risk exposure comes the likely reduction of investment returns. And so diversification is not a panacea, but it is an important principle, albeit one that should be used in moderation. I no longer say, "The more the better." Instead, I point out that to complement the taming effects of diversification, one should also pursue investment balance.

Now a warning: At this point we are going into some detail that you and your advisor will want to discuss together. In fact the rest of this chapter (and the appendix) may be written more for your advisor's benefit. This material will hopefully serve as an aid to your advisor as they explain their reasoning when it comes to their investment recommendations.

Therefore, be patient with yourself as you read the rest of this chapter. It will make better sense to you as your assets increase and your investments become more substantial. In other words, you will want to come back to this material and develop a more thorough understanding as your wealth increases. So, don't give up, you will in fact enjoy some of the upcoming examples, especially the dollar cost averaging game.

The Foundation of Investment Balance

While diversification is important for reducing risk, investment balance has the ability to temper the sacrifice of yield that can result. The objective is to optimize investment yields while minimizing risk exposure; this requires proper balance between different kinds of assets. There are two primary dimensions of balance to be considered. The first dimension addresses conventional investment balance in two broad categories: income assets and growth assets.

INCOME ASSETS (Debt or Lender Assets)	GROWTH ASSETS (Equity or Owner Assets)
Money you "loan" in return for specified interest payments and the eventual return of your principal	Represents "ownership" in the underlying asset with full potential for appreciation and investment earnings

The second dimension of investment balance addresses contemporary investment strategy, which suggests that assets should be divided into three important classes: stable assets, financial assets, and tangible assets (also known as alternative assets).

Stable Assets	Principal remains constant and secure
Financial Assets	Marketable securities with the potential for higher yields
Tangible Assets	Assets with a physical nature

The Asset Balance Matrix®

The blending of these two dimensions results in a dynamic analytical tool: the Asset Balance Matrix® (ABM).

ABM	INCOME ASSETS	GROWTH ASSETS
Stable Assets	Savings Certificates of Deposit Money Market	Index Annuities Index Certificates Index CDs
Financial Assets	Government Bonds Corporate Bonds Municipal Bonds	Stocks Equity Mutual Funds International Securities
Tangible Assets	Mortgage Loans Business Loans Venture Loans	Real Estate Private Placements Alternative Investments

Maintaining investment balance helps reduce the risk of buying high and selling low, a big problem where many people fall prey. The goal instead is to buy low and sell high. Via the balance discipline, we try to harvest gains during times when markets are high (as shown by an out of balance condition) and purchase while markets are low. For a detailed explanation of this discipline and a full description of the Asset Balance Matrix, see Appendix 4 ("Asset Balance Matrix Detail").

Dollar Cost Averaging

A common mistake that investors make is in believing that a down market is always bad. This is only true if you are selling. For those in the accumulation phase, a down market actually represents opportunity. How sad it is to hear about the investor who has been building his portfolio only to find that it has declined significantly during a market downturn and then he makes the critical mistake: he sells.

"After all," Bob reasoned, "I need to cut my losses. I've been investing regularly into this mutual fund that supposedly had a great track record, and it's gone down more than it's gone up. In fact, my account is actually worth less than what I invested!" Bob had been building his portfolio with the discipline of regular monthly investing via his company 401(k) plan, but he lacked an understanding about the nature of investment markets and how to benefit from their fluctuation.

As previously mentioned, the goal is to buy low and sell high. And yet in a moment of panic, Bob sells low, the exact opposite of what he intellectually knows to be the prudent course of action. Why is it that intelligent people make such mistakes? Perhaps it's because of greed and fear. We all know about buy low, sell high. But because of our emotions, we may take the wrong actions.

How sad for Bob: he exited the market at the very moment when it was "the best of times," the time of opportunity— the time when share prices were "on sale." It was a time to be celebrating, not panicking. Sometimes all it takes is access to wise counsel to help us stay the course and keep us focused on the basic principles of investing—one of which is dollar cost averaging, a simple mathematical phenomenon that actually capitalizes on market fluctuations.

> *Now for something really cool: Here is where you might want to slow your reading pace and follow along closely. We are going to get into a few calculations together, but you won't have to do the math. It's done for you; just follow along and enjoy!*

Simply stated, dollar cost averaging (DCA) is the act of placing the same number of dollars into the same portfolio of securities at regular intervals—for example, investing $1,000 per month into a balanced mutual fund.

Because the number of shares that can be bought for a fixed amount of money varies inversely with their price, DCA leads to more shares being bought when their price is low, and a smaller number of shares when they are expensive. As a mathematical result, DCA causes the average *cost* per share of the investments purchased to be lower than the average purchase *price* of those same shares.

At this moment, you're probably asking yourself, "What? How can that be?" The best way to help you come to an understanding of this phenomenon is for us to play a little investing game together.

In this game, you are going to answer yes or no to the idea of investing into a hypothetical mutual fund for a brief, six-month period via dollar cost averaging. The specific question is: Would you invest $1,000 each month for six months into this mutual fund and then sell all your shares at the sixth month's price?

Now, although a real-life investment decision would not have the benefit of knowing the prices for each month in advance, in this game you do have that information. Specifically, the prices are as follows:

Month 1: $5
Month 2: $10
Month 3: $1
Month 4: $10
Month 5: $1
Month 6: $5

If you say yes, then you will be purchasing your shares at a price of $5 in the first month, then $10 in the second month, and so on up to the sixth month, when you will purchase the last of your shares at $5 each. Then you will sell all of your shares at the sixth month's price of $5 and take your profits or losses. Following is a graphical depiction:

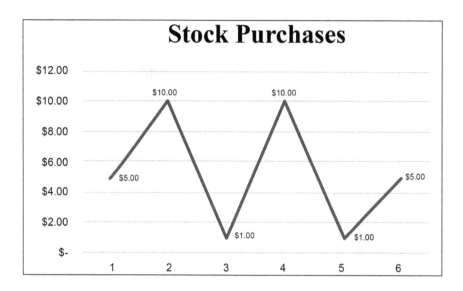

Now, given the benefit of advanced knowledge, knowing precisely what the purchase and sale prices are, it's time to make the decision. Without looking ahead, please make your decision: yes or no?

Would you like to reconsider? Let's do a quick calculation together before you decide again. Let's calculate the average price per share during this six-month period. The math is easy; we simply add each of the prices:

$$\$5+10+1+10+1+5 = 32$$

To determine the average price, we divide this sum by the number of purchases, 6:

$$32\div6 = \$5.33$$

So, knowing that the average purchase price would be $5.33 and the price you will be selling at is $5, what is your thinking now? Yes or no, would you make this investment?

Now let's calculate the outcome of this investment and determine how much profit or loss there actually was. To do this, we first must calculate the number of shares purchased. By dividing the price per share for each month into the $1,000 amount invested, we can calculate the total by adding each result:

$$
\begin{aligned}
\text{Month 1:} \$1,000 \div \$5 &= 200 \\
\text{Month 2:} \$1,000 \div \$10 &= 100 \\
\text{Month 3:} \$1,000 \div \$1 &= 1,000 \\
\text{Month 4:} \$1,000 \div \$10 &= 100 \\
\text{Month 5:} \$1,000 \div \$1 &= 1,000 \\
\text{Month 6:} \$1,000 \div \$5 &= 200 \\
\hline
\text{Total:} &\quad 2,600 \text{ Shares}
\end{aligned}
$$

To calculate the value of these shares, we multiply by the sale price of $5:

$$\$5 \times 2600 = \$13,000$$

To calculate the profit or loss, we must subtract the total investment of $6,000:

$$\$13,000 - 6,000 = \$7,000$$

Wow! How does a go-nowhere investment, which starts at $5 per share and ends at the same value, produce a profit of over 100%? Especially when we know that the average *price* for a share during the period was $5.33 (33 cents higher than the sale price per share)?

The answer is found by finally calculating the average *cost* per share. To do this, we simply divide the total amount invested ($6,000) by the number of shares purchased (2,600):

$$\$6,000 \div 2,600 = \$2.31$$

With an average cost of only $2.31, a sale price of $5.00 will naturally produce a significant profit (over 100%). So as explained earlier, the mathematical consequence of DCA is that the average *cost* per share ends up being less than the average purchase *price* per share. This can substantially improve your potential for profit, even if the investment seemingly goes nowhere—as long as there are fluctuations in value along the way.

Of course, anyone would buy all the shares they could at $2.31 if they knew for sure that they could soon afterward sell them for $5 each. In real life, however, we don't have the luxury of knowing in advance how exactly an investment will perform. Of course, if we do our due diligence in terms of research, we can hopefully have a good idea of an investment's potential.

Real life rarely provides the extreme fluctuations offered in this particular investment game. But hopefully, you can now see how DCA is a simple way for you to take advantage of the fluctuating markets in which you will find your financial investments, namely your stocks, bonds, and mutual funds. If our friend Bob had understood DCA, he might have realized that the down market in which he found himself was actually a wonderful opportunity for him to accumulate a greater proportion of his investment shares, with the potential for greater profit in the future.

Does DCA now make sense to you? To test your understanding, go to appendix 5 ("Dollar Cost Averaging – Game #2") for another investment game with a very interesting twist of reality.

By the way, it would be natural to wonder if a person with a lump sum to invest should wait and DCA instead. History shows that approach to be generally unwise.[16][17] Better to place the lump sum investment in accordance with your ideal Asset Balance Matrix˙ as described earlier.

The benefit of DCA is that it encourages those in the "accumulation" phase (for example, participating in a 401(k) plan) to stay the course during market corrections. These are the times when one can accumulate a disproportionally large number of shares at lower costs, which is the mathematical outcome of DCA.

Please note that it is not appropriate to use a fluctuating investment like a stock or mutual fund for a short-term goal, because you may find the investment down in value at the time you need to sell. If you are accumulating funds for a short-term goal (6–24 months), use a more appropriate stable assets vehicle, like a money market account or savings account. For mid-term goals (25–48 months), use a portfolio of short-term bonds.

For dollar cost averaging to succeed, there must be at least some recovery in the value of the investment, and that can take time. (It doesn't necessarily have to be a full recovery; had the final price been only $4 in our game above, there still would have been a $4,600 profit.) Over the long run, it is reasonable to expect that a balanced, diversified portfolio will recover from a down market. Historically, the markets have always recovered—and made further advances as well (see appendix 6).

Beware Dollar Cost "Ravaging"

Also, one might think that at retirement, a monthly withdrawal from their fluctuating portfolio is appropriate. Wrong. In doing so, a disproportionally large number of shares will be sold at lower prices. This could have a ravaging effect on one's portfolio. Better to utilize a "conduit" money market account that captures extra funds from the gains during the rebalancing of the Asset Balance Matrix˙ to provide retirement income that can be withdrawn.

The Conduit Account

Let's take a moment to discuss further the methodology for drawing retirement income.

During the rebalancing activities of the Asset Balance Matrix,˙ a portion of the harvested gains are placed into a money market or similar stable account (the "conduit" account). From this account, the monthly retirement income is withdrawn, typically in an automated fashion whereby the funds are transferred to the client's checking account on a specified date each month. It is best to limit the withdrawal amount to around 4% of the total portfolio value so that there is opportunity for the portfolio to continue growing. This way, the monthly income received can increase over time to offset the effects of inflation.

During retirement, it is appropriate for the Asset Balance Matrix to be managed more conservatively. Higher proportions should be allocated to the income side of the equation. Also, tangible assets should be gradually diminished because of their higher risk and illiquidity.

If more than a 4% draw rate is desired, careful monitoring of the portfolio is needed in order to make sure that, if principal is invaded, it doesn't jeopardize the portfolio's ability to last for the full life expectancy of the recipient(s).

Annuities

Some people choose to "annuitize" their income by turning over their lump sum investment assets to an insurance company in exchange for an income that will last for the rest of their lives. The insurance salesman can make this idea sound very appealing, but in fact, doing so is rarely a wise decision. While the income may be nice, one must remember that their net worth has now been reduced. When they die, there will be little or nothing left of this account for their heirs or for charity.

Unwary annuitants often don't realize that much of what they were receiving in annuity payments was their own principal. As an alternative, an intelligently balanced investment portfolio should be able to generate the same income with little or no invasion of principal. As a result, there should still be substantial wealth to pass on to heirs and charity in the future.

Enhanced Returns Through Judicious Leverage

With Formula 15 in mind, we have seen the potential for enhanced yields through the Asset Balance Matrix˚ and through dollar cost averaging. Now let's discuss the idea of investment leverage.

Let me start by first saying that leverage involves the use of debt, which can be quite dangerous. Later we'll discuss how ridiculous it is to carry a balance with a credit card company, paying them upwards of 15% or 20%, thus allowing the incredible math of compound interest to work against us instead of for us. So why am I now suggesting the use of debt within our investment pursuits?

The answer lies once again in the simple math of it all. If for example, you contemplate the idea of purchasing a $1,000,000 investment property that has the potential to appreciate at the rate of 5% per year, you might not be too excited about the prospect. Why take the risk and deal with the illiquidity associated with real estate for such a small yield—only 5%? Well, if you finance a portion of the purchase rather than paying cash for the property, the investment return changes quite significantly. Suppose you deploy only $250,000 of your own cash and borrow the other $750,000 from the bank in order to complete the purchase. Rather than only a 5% yield on your investment, your return might be significantly better. Here's the math:

$1,000,000 purchase price Grows to:
$1,250,000 (5 years @ 5%)
− $750,000 (paying off bank after 5 years)
  $500,000 (net proceeds)
Result: $250,000 grows to $500,000—*a 100% profit!*

So instead of generating only a 25% profit over 5 years or 5% per year (simple), you end up with a 100% profit or 20% per year (simple). A significant improvement due to leverage. You can still deploy your full $1 million by purchasing a $4 million property using the same formula, or as an alternative you can purchase four $1 million properties and also benefit from diversification.

Now, once again for the sake of brevity, I have used an over-simplified example and have not yet discussed any of the challenges or the full risk exposure. So let's touch on a few of these. First, you probably noticed that the loan was "interest-only" because the full $750,000 was due when the property sold. The question is: what about that interest—doesn't that subtract from the total investment return? The answer is yes—unless you invest in income property whereby the tenant pays rent sufficient to fully service the loan along with the other expenses of property ownership. Ideally, you as the investor should expect a positive cash flow during the ownership period and should also enjoy all the benefit of the leveraged capital appreciation. Otherwise, the investment should probably be avoided.

Simple versus Compound Interest

Notice also the use of a simple interest calculation in the above example. This was done to keep the math simple and make the basic concept easy to understand. But this might be a good time to discuss the difference between simple and compound interest for purposes of calculating investment yield.

We've discussed the concept of earning compound interest on your savings and investments and the fact that earning interest on interest can produce very large gains over time. If, however, you earned interest only on the original principal invested, then it would be a simple interest return, and a higher rate of return would be required under that scenario to produce the same results.

Following are the simple and compound returns on the above investment examples:

Annual Yields

All Cash
$1,000,000 (5 years) → $1,250,000 = $250,000 growth
Simple interest: 5%
Compound interest: 4.56%

Leveraged
$250,000 (5 years) → $500,000 = $250,000 growth
Simple interest: 20%
Compound interest: 14.87%

As you can see, to produce the All Cash results above it only takes a 4.56% compound return, while to produce the Leveraged results only takes a 14.87% compound return. To put it another way, if you place $1,000,000 into a savings account that pays an annual compound return of 4.56%, you would end up with an account balance of $1,250,000 at the end of five years. And depositing $250,000 into an account paying a 14.87% annual compound return would produce a $500,000 balance in the same time-period. For the sake of comparison, most investment returns are quoted in compound terms, also referred to as Internal Rate of Return (IRR).

There are many other considerations and challenges involved with real estate investments, especially when they are leveraged. For example, what if the value of the property goes down instead of up? A 5% annual reduction in value would wipe out your $250,000 equity entirely if you sold after 5 years. Or what if your tenants move out and you are unable to make the mortgage payments to the bank? Or what if there is a balloon payment and you are unable to secure new financing? The bank will foreclose on the property and take it away from you, resulting in a total loss of your investment. And what if you personally guaranteed the loan? Now the bank can come after your other assets, putting everything you own at risk. Bad idea, don't ever do that.

Because of the above risks, many astute real estate investors work toward having all of their real estate completely free and clear, and any debt that they do have encumbering the real estate is to be non-recourse so they do not become "a servant to the lender." (Prov. 22:7). It is also crucial that you have substantial cash reserves so that you can weather the many unexpected challenges along the way.

What about property management responsibilities? Do you have the time for that, or will the rental income be sufficient to pay for professional property management? Suffice it to say, there is much to consider when making a real estate property investment, and you should seek wise counsel before attempting to make your first purchase.

Hopefully, I haven't frightened you away from the idea of leveraged investing with all of these challenges and considerations. Our family has experienced many favorable investment results over the years, but some of our greatest investment returns have been via tangible investments. We have carefully selected and negotiated a number of real estate investment opportunities over the years, and with the judicious use of leverage, our investment returns have enabled us to execute on Formula 15 and achieve financial independence at a relatively early age.

Oh, and by the way—be very wary about buying into a real estate investment with negative cash flow. You need positive cash flow, with significant potential for expansion of that cash flow, in order to have any expectation of appreciation in market value for future sale purposes. And finally, don't get taken in by the threat that a particular investment opportunity won't last. There's another opportunity every day. Make sure that the purchase deal you make is truly a hot bargain; otherwise, wait till the next one comes along.

Happy and Sad

Ultimately, your investments will bring you many exciting experiences—hopefully good ones for the most part. The reality, however, is that some investments will disappoint. That's to be expected in your financial journey, but if you are diversified and balanced, hopefully the disappointments won't be that significant.

In fact, you may find comfort in knowing that everyone tends to second-guess their investment decisions regardless of whether they go well or not, as in the following parable:

A man traveling through the desert was awakened by an angel in the night. The angel told him to get up and go about collecting stones and placing them in his garments. He complied, and then went back to sleep.

When he awoke in the morning, he was amazed to see that each stone had turned into a precious gem. He was happy for the number of stones he had collected the night before. He was also sad that he hadn't collected more.

And so it goes with our investments: When we make a good investment, we are happy for the amount that we invested, and at the same time sad for not investing more. When an investment performs poorly, we are sad for the amount we did invest, and happy about the amounts we didn't.

Nowadays at the firm, we sometimes abbreviate our reactions to various investment results with a shrug of our shoulders and the expression "happy and sad." With a diversified and biblically responsible approach to investment, you can pursue financial independence with contentment that goes beyond "happy" or "sad." In the next chapter, we will examine several further principles of disciplined and scripturally sound financial management.

WORKBOOK

CHAPTER 3 QUESTIONS

Question: How is investing different from gambling?

_____

_____

_____

_____

_____

_____

_____

_____

Question: What is the logic behind the Asset Balance Matrix? What are some specific steps you might take to create a more balanced asset portfolio for yourself?

_____

_____

_____

_____

_____

_____

_____

_____

Question: What advice in this chapter or the book so far has seemed counterintuitive to you? What does this tell you about wisdom in matters of investment and money management?

_____

_____

_____

_____

_____

_____

_____

_____

_____

_____

_____

Action: Investing is fundamentally different from gambling—which you should be determined to avoid! As a wise investor, prepare for the worst-case scenario with diversification of your assets. Meanwhile, establish a solid financial foundation by maintaining investment balance and using the strategy of dollar cost averaging. And of course, don't underestimate the power of compound interest! Act on the basis of math and wise counsel, not intuition. Then accept with peace of mind that your natural response to your investments will be both "happy and sad."

CHAPTER 3 NOTES

_____
_____
_____
_____
_____
_____
_____
_____
_____
_____
_____
_____
_____
_____
_____
_____
_____
_____
_____
_____
_____
_____
_____
_____

CHAPTER FOUR

Biblically Wise Investing and Money Management

Biblically Responsible Investing (BRI)

Over the years, our family has come under the conviction that our investments should better reflect our faith-based values. Therefore, we now try to avoid certain investments that conflict with biblical values—for example, cigarette companies, gambling, and pornography. Thankfully today there are mutual funds that focus on companies that are a blessing to their customers, their employees, their communities and of course their shareholders. We're comfortable with the possibility that this practice might result in some yield sacrifice. But wouldn't it be reasonable to expect that over the long run, these biblically sound investments will do better financially than those that are detrimental to society?

This is one of several considerations critical to a disciplined approach to investing and managing our finances. Much has already been written on Biblically Responsible Investing (BRI). May I suggest:

- *Investing with Integrity* by Loran Graham, CPA, CFP˚, CKA˚
- *I Found Jesus in the Stock Market* by Cassandra Laymon, CFP˚, CKA˚

Remember this; how you profit, matters.

Budgeting Is Prioritizing

For which of you, desiring to build a tower, does not first sit down and count the cost, whether he has enough to complete it?
— **Luke 14:28 (ESV)**

Let's talk about cash flow management—or we can call it a spending plan. For some reason, many people cringe at the mention of budgeting. Whatever you want to call it, it needs to be done, but it doesn't have to be intimidating. In fact, once you really get into it, you'll find it not only rewarding but also enjoyable at times. And ultimately, once you've established your priorities, it can be quite simple.

Ron Blue's book *Master Your Money* is a must-read on this topic,[18] and the Compass or Crown course that features Howard Dayton's book *Your Money Counts* is a necessity as well. [19] This is a study that will provide all of the stewardship basics, including budgeting. Therefore, I'm not going to say much more in this book about budgeting except that you will benefit from it—so do it.

The topic that isn't emphasized enough elsewhere though, is that of prioritizing. Ultimately, this comes down to knowing whom to pay first: First, pay God in the form of His tithes (10%). Pay yourself in the form of savings and investments toward your financial independence (try to reach 15%). Third, pay everything else as necessary. "Everything else" includes income taxes, mortgage payments or rent, utilities, groceries, property taxes, insurance, charitable giving, clothing, gifts, etc. You can prioritize those as you see fit—and technically, the government might require its cut in the form of taxes before you have the chance to tithe, save, or invest—but for budgeting purposes, the total of such expenses must fit within the 75% not reserved for God and you.

Parkinson's Law

Let's put all of this into perspective by bringing Parkinson's Law into the conversation. Parkinson's Law simply states that your needs will rise to your income. You will notice that over time, as your income increases, many of the things that used to be classified as "wants" will somehow turn into "needs"—the newer car, the kitchen remodel, nicer vacations, etc.

Given this tendency, keep in mind that the great majority of people alive in this world today live a lifestyle nowhere near yours. They have no choice but to adjust their lifestyles to fit within the income that they receive, just as you do. But the average non-American household earns only $9,733 per year. The average American household earns $43,585 per year and spends every bit of it.[20] In fact, many people spend more than their income by going into debt.

Don't ever do that. Figure out a way to live within 75% of your income. Never allow credit card balances to go unpaid. In other words, if you can't pay off your credit card entirely at the end of the month, you should not be using the card. Don't make discretionary purchases unless you are certain that you'll have the cash to cover those purchases this month. If you don't, wait till next month. These are what we call disciplines.

It's possible that as you're reading this, you're realizing you've already established a lifestyle that exceeds 75% of your income and you're wishing that you had established these disciplines earlier. Take heart. Parkinson's Law works in reverse as well. If you were to take a 25% pay cut, you would figure out a way to adjust your lifestyle to fit within your new income level. Likewise, as you establish the disciplines of tithing and investing first, you will figure out a way to fit your lifestyle within the remaining 75%. Perhaps you'll have to phase into it (baby steps), but don't delay—start those steps today!

"But Grandpa, I just can't do that—my income isn't high enough!" Perhaps I didn't sufficiently emphasize the contrast of your lifestyle versus the other 99% of people in this world. Visit GlobalRichList.com, and enter your country and annual income. You'll find that if your income is at least $32,500 per year, you're in the top 1% worldwide!

Yes, the cost of living in your country might be higher than in other countries. But understanding that 99% of people in this world today live on less than $32,500 per year can provide useful perspective. You *can* live within your means!

Automation

One way to establish and maintain the discipline of investing toward your financial independence is to automate the process. If you can establish a payroll deduction arrangement with your employer, that may work best. Just as your employer withholds income taxes from your payroll, it's likely they can also deduct part of your income for your savings. Of course, if it's available, you should participate in their sponsored retirement plan, such as a 401(k). Don't miss out on that opportunity. Not only will it function as a good aid to your priority discipline, but it may also function as a great head start on your investment returns.

Consider this: most employers offer a matching arrangement, typically 50% of the amount that you save, up to perhaps 6% of your income. This means that if you earn $5,000 per month and agree to a 6% participation level in your employer's 401(k), you'll be investing $300 per month into your future. But it won't actually cost you $300, because the deduction from your income occurs before income taxes. For example, if you are in a 30% tax bracket (state and federal), your net reduction in take-home pay is only $210.

Yet you're putting $300 to work for you, right? Wrong. Actually, because the employer matches 50% of that amount, $450 is put to work for you. That's better than a 100% gain right from the start! I don't know of any other investment opportunity that will grow a $210 investment to $450 on day one. This can be a great jump-start to your efforts in seeking the higher investment returns needed for a Formula 15-type plan for financial independence.

And yet you would be amazed at how many intelligent people I've encountered over the years who have willfully selected not to participate in their company 401(k) plan. I'm incredulous each time, and I tell them so. Recent US tax data reveals that 79% of Americans work at places that sponsor a 401(k)-style plan, and yet only 41% of those workers actually participate.[21] Incredible! Don't make the mistake of delaying your participation in your employer-sponsored retirement plan.

Another form of automation is an ACH bank arrangement in which your investment account (brokerage account, mutual fund account, etc.) is authorized to draw a set amount from your checking account each month on the date that you specify. Knowing that this monthly transfer of funds is going to occur will help in establishing and maintaining this important saving discipline.

There will be times when you might feel a bit stressed as you contemplate your expenses for the month, and you may secretly wish that ACH arrangement wasn't there. Actually, you can stop or reduce it at any time, but you likely won't. It will seem too much of a bother to contact the firm or mess with your computer to make the change, and instead you'll just make the budget work somehow. And that's exactly what we want to happen—one of the few times inertia (inaction) can be your friend.

Never a Convenient Time

There is never a convenient time to start saving. A person can come up with many reasons not to start or continue a savings or investment plan:

"It's January and I need a month or so to recover from the heavy holiday spending... It's March and tax season is just around the corner—I'd better wait till after I pay property taxes and know the outcome of potential income tax obligations... It's May, time to plan for vacation... It's July, I'm on vacation... It's September and we have back-to-school expenses... It's November and the holidays are here..."

Remember, needs are different from wants. Wants can become perceived as needs. You can defer gratification by putting off a purchase for a while, but putting off your plans of financial independence exacts a significant cost.

The Cost of Waiting

It's better late than never when it comes to taking advantage of the principle of compounding interest, but there is a substantial cost to waiting when it comes to wealth building. Let's look at the example of a 30-year-old who has invested in an Individual Retirement Account (IRA):

Basic IRA example. Save $5,500 at the beginning of each year for 35 years and average a 10% yield. The IRA account will grow to $1,639,697.

Impressive. Now suppose this 30-year-old had decided to delay just one year: saving $5,500/year for 34 years and averaging a 10% yield results in the account growing to $1,485,134.

That's a difference of $154,563 for waiting only one year.

Now divide that by 12: delaying for only one month costs $12,880.

Therefore, time is clearly the most important of the three components (savings amount, yield, and time) within the financial independence formula that we described earlier. Take advantage of your youth and those precious beginning years, when investments will accumulate much more interest earnings than the amounts invested in later years. The bottom line is: do not wait. Waiting even one year will shrink your final retirement sum substantially. To see the full math on this, go to appendix 7 ("The Cost of Waiting One Year").

Variable Income Business Account

Many people live on a variable income because they are independent contractors or self-employed. Or perhaps part of your income comes in the form of commissions or bonuses. It's difficult to manage your cash flow when you're not certain how much income you'll receive each month. The solution for this is to establish a "business account" which will receive the various forms of income. From the business account you should then pay yourself a reasonable fixed salary into your household account. Ideally the business account should accumulate some reserves so that your salary won't be interrupted during the lean times.

Now that you have a consistent income arriving into your household account, you can better plan your budget and there's no need for frequent adjustments of your lifestyle.

Six Basics of Responsible Money Management

Earlier I mentioned the importance of seeking wise counsel for your finances. When doing so, consider finding someone who shares your biblical worldview if possible. This is the purpose of Kingdom Advisors, an organization that equips financial professionals with scriptural wisdom above and beyond their technical, secular training.

Accordingly, there are six fundamental principles of money and money management that every Certified Kingdom Advisor˙ (CKA˙) knows:

- Spend less than you earn
- Avoid the use of debt
- Build liquidity
- Set long-term goals
- Remember that God owns it all
- Rejoice in generosity

I'd like to expound a little on each of these principles.

1. Spend Less Than You Earn

You have likely heard people say, "Live within your means." But frankly, that is insufficient. You should live *below* your means; that is, spend less than you earn. This will enable you to save the difference and build for your future. Over the years, you will amass substantial wealth if you follow this simple discipline.

We discussed earlier that prioritizing your spending within your budget is important. Specifically, pay God (His 10% tithe), pay yourself (save and invest 15%), and then pay everyone else. As I emphasized before, it *is* possible to adjust your lifestyle to live within the remaining 75% of your income.

To put it simply, spend less than you earn and save the rest for a long time.

We live in an entitlement society that is constantly bombarded with advertisements that tell us we deserve a better lifestyle. The advertisers even suggest that it's okay to go into debt and spend more than we earn. Following this thinking can ruin your life—thus the next principle we'll discuss.

2. Avoid the Use of Debt

Just as the rich rule the poor, so the borrower is servant to the lender. — **Proverbs 22:7 (ESV)**

Bottom line, be an interest receiver, not an interest payer. We covered the concept of compound interest earlier; over time it will amass a fortune. Interest compounding is what makes lenders so profitable. Credit card companies in particular, at rates of 15–20% or more, can essentially extract the financial hopes and dreams of their customers in exchange for the immediate gratification of an unwise purchase.

Do not buy anything with a credit card that you cannot afford to pay off entirely when the bill arrives. Think of this: there are people out there who are still making payments on a pizza they ate years ago. If you allow a credit card balance to go unpaid, you are making the power of compound interest work against you instead of for you. Therefore, keep your lifestyle adjusted so that your spending is below your income, sufficient to keep all consumer purchases paid this month. It is much less difficult to delay a purchase temporarily today than to suffer the financial consequences of an unwise, premature purchase over the long term.

I hate it when an author keeps repeating himself, but I can't apologize for repeating this particular point. It simply has too important an impact on your life. My colleague Jon Rehurek is writing a book on stewardship,[22] and he has a list of "non-negotiables" when it comes to credit card use:

1. Only purchase items that you *already* have the money to pay for within your budget. Avoid purchasing impulse items on credit, even though this can be challenging.

2. Pay off the balance *entirely every* month prior to your payment due date (i.e., *never* pay just the minimum payment and *never* carry a balance).

3. Never incur interest.

4. Don't spend any more than you would spend if using cash or debit cards. Studies show that most people tend to spend *more* when using a credit card then when using cash or a debit card. If you find yourself doing this—*and most likely you will spend more when using a credit card*—stop using credit cards. For the typical person, it is more difficult to make a purchase if he or she knows that the money is coming out of his or her checking account *directly* and *immediately* versus the credit mentality that says, "I can pay this off later."

Because many financial counselors hold the view that there is no such thing as "responsible credit card use," these principles are recommended *only* for those with iron-clad discipline. All others should perform "plastic surgery" on their credit cards and cut them up.

Now, I realize that some reading this book, being previously unaware of these disciplines, may find themselves carrying a balance on one or more credit cards and unable to pay them off. For you, financial independence is going to require a more significant adjustment to your lifestyle. First, you'll need to make an adjustment to reign in your spending to fit within (actually, below) your income.

Second, you'll have to limit your lifestyle further to pay for your earlier purchases and the accompanying interest. When you take the Compass course at your church, you will learn how to "snowball" your credit card balances by concentrating larger monthly payments on one account at a time (while also servicing other debts) to knock down one account after the other. To get a head start, go to Sean Freiburg's Unbury loan calculator (www.unbury.us) and experiment with different scenarios to see your potential interest savings.

Regarding other forms of consumer debt: if possible, wait to purchase your first car until you can do it with cash. Easier said than done, I realize; perhaps you need a car to get you to your job. If you must finance that first car, buy a sensible used car, not a new one. Make the largest down payment possible and finance it for the shortest possible time. Once paid off, keep the car and keep making those payments, not to the lender but into your savings account. Eventually, you'll be able to buy all of your cars with cash.

Now the tough one: your home. Few people ever get to the point where they own their home debt-free, but it is possible. Here too, be sensible when buying your first home, and when you can afford to do so, make larger payments on your mortgage than required. That entire extra amount applies fully to principal and can significantly reduce the time it takes to pay it off.

3. Build Liquidity

Precious treasure and oil are in a wise man's dwelling, but a foolish man devours it. — **Proverbs 21:20 (ESV)**

It's one thing to have all kinds of great investments and to pay cash for your things, but without adequate reserves, you might find yourself in trouble. Not all investments go as planned. What if your stocks are down at a time when you need some emergency cash? What if your leveraged real estate investment loses its tenant? If you don't have adequate reserves, you'll be unable to service the mortgage. The lender has a lien on that property and will take it from you to satisfy that lien. Now you've lost your property, the money you invested, and your credit rating.

Or what if you lose your job? How will you cover your monthly expenses? The rule of thumb is to have 3–6 months' worth of expenses in liquid reserves, whether it be for your business or your household.

Moreover, what if you encounter a hot investment opportunity? This and many other reasons justify holding cash reserves despite their low-yield nature. Make sure you have enough.

Accumulating reserves should come naturally because God has set the instinct of savings within all of His creations. The simple ants gather and store; the squirrel stores away acorns for the time when food is scarce. Have a plan for storing liquid reserves in a consistent manner.

4. Set Long-Term Goals

The heart of man plans his way, but the LORD establishes his steps. — **Proverbs 16:9 (ESV)**

The other day, I heard the proverb, "Man plans and God laughs," and it occurred to me that at times He likely weeps instead. Nevertheless, it is rare that you will meet a successful person and learn he achieved something that wasn't his goal. Perhaps it started in his imagination, as merely a dream for the future. But as he thought more about it, the dream evolved into a goal and then a plan.

For as he thinks within himself, so he is. — **Proverbs 23:7 (NASB)**

There's an old presentation by Earl Nightingale that addresses what he called "the strangest secret."[23] In it, he explains that you will ultimately become what you think about most of the time.

Sadly, most people never really plan, or if they do, it's only on a superficial level. Imagine agreeing to fly with a private pilot who, when asked about the destination, says, "Oh, I don't know, I figure we'll just fly until our fuel runs out and see where we end up." That's a journey that will likely end in disaster when you run out of fuel at a place that doesn't have an airport.

Planning for long-term goals gives you a target to hit that will make your future years better. Scripture offers a balanced approach to setting goals that includes making plans, yet doing so with wisdom and humility. We're to avoid two extremes: (1) never setting goals and (2) setting goals with no thought of God. The balanced alternative is found in James 4:15 (ESV): "Instead you ought to say, 'If it is the Lord's will, we will live and do this or that.'" It's good to make plans as long as we seek God's will along the way and leave room for Him to change them. His goals take precedence over ours.

Let's go back to your journey with the private pilot, whom you've convinced to set a destination. His next step is to take inventory of where you're at right now and then determine a course or heading that will take you to your goal. This procedure applies not only to one's travels, but also to the financial planning process, during which a financial inventory is taken and then a plan is established that will take you to your ultimate objectives. Once you're underway, the winds of change will be encountered and course corrections will ultimately be needed in order to reach your destination.

5. Remember That God Owns It All

Everything in the heavens and earth is yours O Lord and this is your kingdom. We adore you as being in control of everything. Riches and honor come from you alone and you are the ruler of all mankind; your hand controls power and might, and it is at your discretion that men are made great and given strength. — *1* ***Chronicles 29:11–12 (ESV)***

The above scripture says it all. It all belongs to God. The sooner in life we recognize the difference between our stewardship role and God's ownership, the better. With this as our perspective, we can view our possessions differently. Now we recognize that they are to be managed in the best interests of the owner. Our ultimate objective is to hear His wonderful words:

Well done, good and faithful servant. You have been faithful over a little; I will set you over much. Enter into the joy of your master. — ***Matthew 25:21 (ESV)***

6. Rejoice in Generosity

Developing the joy of generosity is of immense importance, but it does not seem to come naturally to most people—it certainly didn't for me. But as we begin to consider what really brings us joy, it turns out to be a function of how we can be a blessing to others. If we can do so with a portion of our wealth, we begin to understand God's purpose in blessing us with it in the first place.

God blesses us so we can bless others; in my experience, the more generous we are with others, the more God seems to be generous with us. Although the personal reward of generosity should not be our motivation, it turns out that ultimately we can't avoid it—both in terms of material rewards and also, importantly, in the form of greater joy.

Skin in the Game

Whether you're considering a charitable investment or an investment in a new financial asset, a good question to ask someone who is trying to get you to invest in something is, "Have you put your own money in this investment?" If the answer is no, the next step might be to inquire as to why his proposed investment is appropriate for your money but not for his. At our firm, we welcome investment ideas from others, and it's very important for us to know that the person promoting the idea has "skin in the game" along with us. Likewise, the other families that invest with us like to know that we have our money invested in the same opportunities as they do.

In fact, I have found that this concept goes a long way in other aspects of life. My wonderful dad, Vince Sanada, Jr., was a hardworking man, and he provided well for our family. However, there wasn't enough money to buy me a car or to pay for my college education. So I bought my own car, and I worked to put myself through college. As a result, I took good care of that car and studied hard to get good grades—because I had skin in the game. If Dad had offered to pay for these things, I would have gladly accepted, but I'm better off today because he didn't. Yes, it was difficult for me, but it was also character-building (and with all those responsibilities, I had less time to get into trouble).

Sometimes, if you give your children too much, you enable them to be irresponsible. It's better for them to have skin in the game—to have a personal stake in the matter. If you're invested in something, you're going to perform better. I tried to apply this principle with my sons, starting with the purchase of their bicycles. It seemed to me (not to them) that it would be better if they earned at least some of the money toward the purchase.

Therefore, they all learned to earn money from an early age by taking on extra chores around the house and getting good report cards from school (yes, I rewarded them financially for getting good grades). To expedite his bike purchase, Randy Jr. decided to start his own little business. He would go around knocking on doors, "Can I take your trash barrels out and bring them back in for you?" He earned a little extra money and that helped pay for his bicycle.

But when his friends received new cars for their sixteenth birthdays, Randy figured it would be the same for him. What a disappointment when his birthday came, despite the fact that we had told him he would be required to earn at least half of the money toward the purchase of his car. I don't know who suffered more over this decision, Randy Jr. or his mom and me. It's not like we didn't have the money to completely pay for his car; it was the principle of the matter.

Randy was undaunted, though. He got a job bussing tables at a local Italian restaurant, and another one on weekends teaching snowboarding. Not long after, we bought that first car together—and yes, he took very good care of it. We later went through the same process with his three brothers.

As college approached for each of them, my sons knew of my history and knew they would be required to pay for their own college educations. There was a problem here though: college was dramatically more expensive now than in my time. So together we devised our special plan...

The Family College Reimbursement Scholarship

The plan was simple: instead of being required to pay for their entire college education, they needed only to save up enough to cover their first semester. At the end of the semester, we would look together at the grades they had earned. Based on those grades, they received a scholarship whereby I would reimburse their cost of tuition and books proportionate to their performance. For each class in which they earned a C, they would receive 50% of the cost for that class. For every B they would receive 100%, and for every A the reimbursement was 150%. They actually had the potential of making a profit by doing well in school!

And profit they did. By getting mostly A's, they were able to support a decent lifestyle while being able to concentrate on their studies rather than having to seek employment with long work hours. It cost me more than just paying the college expenses outright, but it was one of the best investments I ever made. It's important to remember, however, that we didn't surprise them with this arrangement as they were getting ready to start college. They knew well in advance and developed a work ethic early in order to have most of the funds needed.

Now, not everything works out as planned, and sure enough, one of our sons didn't have sufficient funds saved for the first semester. So we set up a low-interest loan for which he agreed to be responsible. Over time, he was able to repay the loan fully with the profits earned from his grades and some earnings from part-time employment.

All of this required a lot of effort from our sons and also from their mom and me. But we all believe today that it was worth it, in light of how well it worked out. Our four sons received their bachelor degrees (three with honors) with no college debt hanging over their heads. Only Joe, our youngest, took on some debt afterward in order to earn his Juris Doctorate law degree. Of course, that is now fully paid as well. The family college reimbursement scholarship turned out to be a great arrangement, enabled by the effective principle of "skin in the game."

The Inheritance with Skin in the Game

What if you found out that there was a significant inheritance waiting for you, but that you would be required to have skin in the game to receive it? My brother-in-law has an idea to do this that warrants mention here.

He wants to encourage his sons to save for their futures. As they do, we are designing a special trust that will match, dollar for dollar, all of the funds they have accumulated for their financial independence. Wow, what a blessing for them, and what a great incentive!

There's so much more that I'd like to share, but this single volume is not enough to contain a lifetime of financial knowledge.

And so, let me refer you once again to the works of the following authors who serve as my mentors in the area of stewardship:

- *Master Your Money* by Ron Blue, co-founder of Kingdom Advisors
- *Your Money Counts* by Howard Dayton, founder of Compass and Crown
- *Money, Possessions, and Eternity* by Randy Alcorn

Work Works

The need to make sure everyone has skin in the game derives in part from the fact that there are two kinds of people in this world: There are make-it-happen people and there are make-excuses people. People who make a lot of excuses typically do not make things happen. As immigrants, my grandparents proved themselves to be make-it-happen people, and therefore it is part of my heritage—and yours as well.

> *Whatever you do, work heartily, as for the Lord and not for men.*
> — **Colossians 3:23 (ESV)**

The Bible takes a hard stand on people who just try to "get by" and feed off of others without making an effort to work.

> *If anyone is not willing to work, let him not eat—*
> **Thessalonians 3:10 (ESV)**

Notice that it doesn't say, "Those who are unable to work should not eat." We should have compassion and help out those people. But if someone can work, yet will not, then he's left to the consequences of his actions (or inactions, in this case). Your odds of creating wealth increase substantially when you work.

A slack hand causes poverty, but the hand of the diligent makes rich. — **Proverbs 10:4 (ESV)**

Work works. This was the slogan that drove my son Chad's winning football team in high school. And the division manager who hired me at IDS American Express, Gale Parrack, once told me a simple, closely related phrase that has stuck with me all of these years: "Don't worry, work." He knew that we young recruits would be going through some worrisome times. The financial services industry is hard-driving and goal-oriented, but he told us to work, not worry. The time and energy you invest in worrying could be invested in working and getting results instead. When you work, things happen, and soon there's little left to worry about.

Consider the idea of chores. Parents don't assign chores to you because they're mean or because they're trying to get you to do their work for them. In fact, it's often easier to do something yourself than to convince and train an uncooperative person to do it. Rather, parents have the responsibility of imparting a work ethic to their children.

A note to Mom & Dad — perhaps not all chores should be for money. Each family member should pick up after themselves and should be willing to carry their share of the other work around the household. That said, there are certain extra chores deserving of financial compensation, especially if the work produces some value or reduces some expense.

Work works. The simple fact of the matter is, when you're working, you're energized—you're feeling a sense of accomplishment. Perhaps it's not as much as you'd hoped; maybe counterproductive things occur in the course of a day. Maybe you go backward sometimes. Maybe you're being tackled here and there—but buckle down. Work on something. You'll feel better having worked than you would have felt sitting around worrying about things, many of which are beyond your control. We were created to work because we were created in God's image and He is a worker.

We should have the right attitude toward our work:

> *So I saw that there is nothing better than that a man should rejoice in his work...* — **Ecclesiastes 3:22 (ESV)**

We should celebrate and savor our accomplishments:

> *There is nothing better for a person than that he should eat and drink and find enjoyment in his toil. This also, I saw, is from the hand of God.* — **Ecclesiastes 2:24 (ESV)**

If you haven't seen the movie *The Ultimate Gift*, I encourage you to do so. It's the story of a wise and benevolent grandfather (played by James Garner) who recognizes that he must impart important principles to his grandson, including a work ethic, to prepare him for his inheritance.

Be Content, Not Complacent

When I enrolled in the Crown course of study, I glanced at the outline of topics we would be covering. One in particular raised my eyebrow: contentment. I thought that was a bad word. But the Apostle Paul apparently thought otherwise:

> *For I have learned to be content in whatever circumstances I am. I know how to get along with humble means, and I also know how to live in prosperity; in any and every circumstance I have learned the secret of being filled and going hungry, both of having abundance and suffering need. I can do all things through Him who strengthens me.* — **Philippians 4:11–13 (NASB)**

There's a fundamental difference between being content and being complacent. Contentment is a state of being where you accept the reality of your situation, without complaint or resentment. When you're content, you work on the things you can change and accept the things you can't, all the while refusing to be disheartened. You don't let circumstances steal your joy.

When you're complacent, however, you adopt a "good enough" or "that'll do" mentality. You become satisfied with mediocrity, possessing no real aspirations to do and be more.[24]

So the goal is to achieve contentment, which does not come easy for many people, including me. Perhaps we can take comfort in the Apostle Paul's acknowledgment that contentment is something that can be learned.

Hopefully by now you realize that there is much more to financial independence than just the mindless accumulation of wealth. Sadly, not everyone does. Consider the miserable rich people you hear about. "Miserable rich people"—shouldn't that be a contradiction in terms? Shouldn't a person who is financially independent be happy and joyful? Let's address meaningful wealth via financial freedom in the next chapter.

WORKBOOK

CHAPTER 4 QUESTIONS

Question: Where are your spending and investment priorities? How can you adjust your budget to make sure that your priorities are properly addressed?

_____

_____

_____

_____

_____

_____

_____

_____

Question: What is the biggest challenge you face in terms of living within your means and saving/investing money now? What are some possible ways to overcome this challenge?

_____

_____

_____

_____

_____

_____

Question: What does it mean for you to have skin in the game? How can you benefit if others have skin in the game?

_____

_____

_____

_____

_____

_____

_____

_____

_____

Action: Take the necessary measures to abide by the basic principles of biblically responsible money management; otherwise, your financial dreams almost certainly won't come to fruition. Plan a budget that places God first while leaving room for God to work. Reevaluate your "needs" to see which ones are truly "wants" so you can live fully within your means (and still having breathing room). Accordingly, avoid debt like the plague, and work your way out of it as quickly as possible. As you save money, develop liquid cash reserves for opportunities and emergencies. Meanwhile, when you invest, make sure everyone has skin in the game.

Parents - Consider some form of the Family College Reimbursement Scholarship when it comes to college tuition for your kids, and address their inheritance with the same principles in mind. And at all times, remind yourself and your family that "work works," and be content with what you have, but not complacent in what you've already accomplished.

CHAPTER 4 NOTES

_____
_____
_____
_____
_____
_____
_____
_____
_____
_____
_____
_____
_____
_____
_____
_____
_____
_____
_____
_____
_____
_____
_____

Giving Joyfully and Achieving Financial Freedom

Growing up in a Christian home, I came to understand that obedience was important. I didn't initially appreciate the idea of paying tithes; I wanted to add money to my savings account, not the offering plate. I paid tithes out of obedience, not out of desire. Initially I missed the joy in giving, but God gives joyfully and we should too.

My giving started out of obedience, but would be the gateway to something wonderful. It was the beginning of a journey that would bring me to a place of joy I never imagined. As it turns out, the tithe was just the beginning.

The Tithe—Grandma's Ultimate Financial Lesson

The most important financial lesson that my grandma taught me was the concept of tithing. She called me one day to tell me that she was coming to town for a visit. She said, "I want us to have some time together. I have a very important financial principle out of the Bible that I want to teach you." I was around 12 years old. I had a paper route and I was making a lot of money for my age. When she told me this news on the phone, I was really excited because she was the one who had taught me about compound interest. I figured that if she had something important from the Bible about money, then well, this just might be the best investment recommendation ever!

When she arrived, Grandma sat me down and said, "Okay we're going to talk about this money you make from your paper route, and here's what the Bible has to say." She proceeded to explain about the 10% tithe; we are to honor God by giving back to Him the first 10% of our income.

My smiling face disappeared. I thought, "Really? I have to give my money away?" This was not the hot investment idea that I was expecting, but I understood that this was a function of obedience, not just to her but to God. She promised that in time I would come to understand what a blessing this would be for me. I began practicing the discipline of tithing. From everything I made, 10% went into the offering plate at church.

My paper route continued growing, substantially. I was making good money for my age and I was putting what I considered to be a lot into the offering plate. Then I got to thinking, "I'm just a kid, and this is way too much money for someone my age to put in." So I decided, "I'm going to put half the amount in the offering plate." Not long after that they cut my paper route in half. I don't know how much of that was God's specific intervention but it was a great lesson for me. I shaped up and never stopped tithing—I should say almost never. There were a couple of times in my young adulthood when I was a little lax in it, but I got over that pretty quickly.

And Grandma was right again. What a blessing it was for me. God blessed the work of my hands and gave me favor over the years in my employment activities and in my investments. I've never had to seek a job. I achieved and exceeded my financial plans. The interesting thing is, I've never drawn an especially large income from my employment or business activities. It seemed better to reinvest in the business and make sure that our employees were well paid. After all, they have always been such a blessing to me and to our clients, how could I not want to bless them?

So then, how is it that the Sanada Estate has come to the size that it is today? Well, this is where the simple math (which I've relied on for the various formulas in this book) fails to provide an explanation. Is it possible that wealth can increase even as one honors the principle of the tithe?

"Test Me in This"

> *Bring the full tithe into the storehouse, that there may be food in my house. And thereby put me to the test, says the* LORD *of hosts, if I will not open the windows of heaven for you and pour down for you a blessing until there is no more need.* — **Malachi 3:10 (ESV)**

There is no other place in the Bible where it suggests that you try testing God.

Is it possible that the discipline of tithing brings abundant blessing? What a silly question, given this verse in Malachi. I'm not suggesting that you tithe so that you can get more for yourself. That's the wrong attitude and motivation. So I'll simply say to you in the same way that Grandma said it to me, "Honor God's instruction with your tithe and in time you will come to understand what a blessing it will be for you."

While speaking to groups about tithing over the years, I've asked on a number of occasions for people to please let me know if they have practiced this discipline and regretted it. No one ever has. From my own personal experience and the experience of others that I have known, I have come to the belief that the outcome of this tithing discipline transcends the laws of mathematics when it comes to long-term financial results.

Perhaps another way to look at it is: "Test me in this: you will need more storage." Interesting.

Here are some questions that you'll probably think of or hear others asking on this topic:

Tithing was an Old Testament concept—so does it apply to us today? The purpose of tithing is so "that you may learn to revere the LORD your God always" (Deuteronomy 14:23 NIV). One reason God created the concept was to support those serving in His church (the Levites in Old Testament times). The church is every bit as valid today as it was then. Also, it seems to me that if it were no longer applicable, then the practice would result in personal financial loss in direct proportion to the amount given (as the laws of mathematics would suggest). Instead, it somehow produces great increase and rewards.

Does it have to be 10% of all our income to the Lord? "Tithe" literally means "a tenth."

Do we give the Lord tithes based on gross income or net income after taxes? I can certainly understand that question, which I struggled with personally (I'm a slow learner). You'll recall that when Grandma first taught me about tithing, it wasn't very well received on my part. In fact, you can probably surmise that I was not what you would consider to be a "cheerful giver."

And so in my early employment years, I justified in my mind that it was sufficient to tithe on the net. And God blessed me, sufficiently. But I was still only paying the tithe out of obedience and I rarely gave beyond the calculated 10%, other than for an occasional special purpose for the church (like a building fund) or to help support missions in a modest way. Actually, it wasn't until Kay and I took the Crown course that my heart began to comprehend the joy of generosity and I changed to paying on the gross income.

And it wasn't me who came up with the idea of paying the tithe on our firm's gross revenues, it was my sons, Randy Jr. and Jerry. But when they proposed this during one of our strategic planning meetings, my heart leaped for joy. They had already surpassed my own convictions about tithing, and it was with great joy that we sought more fully to live out these words of Jesus:

> *Give and it will be given to you. A good measure, pressed down, shaken together and running over, will be poured into your lap. For with the measure you use, it will be measured to you.* —
> **Luke 6:38 (NIV)**

And we never looked back!

God's Math—the Law of Multiplication

"You cannot out-give God," you'll hear people say throughout your life. Give to God what you are supposed to and it will be multiplied back to you. This is one of those natural laws that cannot be refuted, like the law of gravity.

Perhaps the math isn't about simple addition, but multiplication. You can plant one-third of a bushel of corn and it will yield 30 bushels of corn. This is a natural function of sowing and reaping, and considering it may help us put the results of tithing into perspective. But in reality, the sowing and reaping outcome from the tithe defies logical explanation. It transcends the math we learned in school.

No doubt you are familiar with the passage in the Gospel of Mark where a few loaves and fishes miraculously multiplied and fed thousands of people. There's also a story in the Old Testament about a widow who desperately needed financial help experiencing a miracle of flowing oil from a single jar that filled every vessel she and her sons could find. Selling that oil supplied the provision she needed (see 2 Kings 4:1–7). Suffice it to say, you won't be the first to experience miraculous increase.

The Joy of Generosity

Yet it seems to me that we are typically born selfish. Consider that young children, first learning to speak, tend to say "mine" before "yours" or "ours." For many people, generosity is not natural. My wife, Kay, is an exception; she's always been quite generous. "Perhaps to a fault" was my view in the early years of our marriage. She was undaunted, though, and continued being blessed in her giving as she also served as a good role model for me. For many people, however, generosity is an attribute that needs developing; it is a journey. And that was the case for me.

Here's how it perhaps goes for the typical person: First, you start with obedience, honoring the tithe. Then you hear a missions appeal and begin providing some support. Then, as you really start tiptoeing along the generosity journey, you find yourself committed in a small way to the monthly support of an orphan.

You start thinking about and praying about that child, and begin to realize the difference you're making. You think, "Wow, I'm actually being rewarded here in the joy of what I'm doing for that other person."

Then you find yourself attending a garden party fundraiser benefiting local women and children who have become homeless. As you see their faces and hear their stories, you realize that you are now coming to the aid of widows and orphans, the sweet spot of biblical guidance in our giving. There's a new motivation in your life, a purpose. You're making a critical difference in the lives of others and it feels wonderful. You have found how wealth can bring joy not through the purchase of more things and experiences, but in the blessing of others.

For instance, remember when you were young and it was Christmas morning? Remember the excitement of receiving gifts? What joy that was! But then as we mature, we find ourselves drawing greater joy from the giving than the receiving. As a parent, it's more enjoyable to watch the kids open their gifts than to open your own gifts. We get that, but it takes some maturity to get there. It's the same way in our charitable giving.

Recall the words of the Lord Jesus—that He Himself said, "It is more blessed to give than to receive" (Acts 20:35 ESV).

Giving from Income or Giving from Assets?

I remember the day when my friend Ron Blue, Founding Director of Kingdom Advisors and best-selling author of *Master Your Money*, suggested that there was another dimension of philanthropy besides giving from income. He introduced us Kingdom Advisors to the idea of giving from assets.

Wow! I hadn't ever considered that idea, at least not during lifetime giving. But here he was challenging us to take it to another level, and honestly, I was a bit intimidated. Spiritual giants like Ron Blue, Larry Burkett, and Howard Dayton might be up to such a thing, but I wasn't there yet. Nevertheless, the idea was now permanently embedded in my mind. I mentioned it to Kay and of course she thought it was a great idea.

Giving from assets? I thought assets were to be accumulated for the future—my future. Was that so wrong? Wasn't giving from income enough? Sure it was. After all, we were certainly being blessed enough. What more could we really ask for? I needed some time for all this to register.

Then I read the book *The Eternity Portfolio* by Alan Gotthardt (a fellow Kingdom Advisor) and was reminded that my future consisted of much more than my brief lifetime here on earth. [25] That book served as a great reminder that building treasures on earth is of minimal value in comparison to the rewards we could be accumulating in heaven.

So there's benefit from the account that's building for us in heaven, and we are also getting tremendous joy now from giving. Not a bad combination—but wait, there's more!

Tax Benefits

Current tax laws provide significant benefits for charitable giving. Specifically, amounts given are a write-off against taxable income. There are even greater benefits when giving long-term assets that have appreciated in value since the time when they were purchased.

Let's say you own 1,000 shares of a publicly traded company that you bought for $5,000 and that are now worth $50,000.

If you sell the shares, you will face a federal capital gains tax on your $45,000 gain, typically $15\% \times \$45,000 = \$6,750$ tax. Note that currently, long-term capital gains (LTCG) are taxed at a lower rate than ordinary income.

Perhaps you'd like to sell the shares because you feel that it's time to harvest those gains, and you'd also like to use the after-tax proceeds ($\$50,000 - 6,750 = \$43,250$) to help fund your charitable giving. The full amount of the gift is deductible against your ordinary income, example: $28\% \times \$43,250 = \$12,110$ tax savings. Under this arrangement, the tax savings from the charitable contribution will more than offset the LTCG tax on the sale of the shares. Here's the math:

$12,110 (tax saved by charitable contribution)
− $6,750 (LTCG tax on sale of shares)
  $5,360 (net tax savings)

Not bad, but the better solution is to donate the shares directly to the charity rather than selling them yourself. By doing so, you benefit in three ways:

You get to take a charitable deduction at the fair market value of those shares—$50,000. Taxes saved: 28% x $50,000 = $14,000.

In addition, you won't owe a penny of capital gains tax on that $45,000 gain. The gain is instead assumed by the charity, but because they're tax-exempt, no tax is owed. LTCG taxes owed: $0.

The value of those shares is removed from your estate— reducing your potential exposure to estate taxes.

Now, since there is no taxable gain recognized on the sale of the shares, you now have two tax savings; the charitable deduction and the elimination of the LTCG tax. Here's the math:

$14,000 (taxes saved by charitable contribution)
− $0 (LTCG tax on sale of shares)
$14,000 (net tax savings)

Net tax savings are much more than double! Plus, the charity receives a full $50,000 instead of the net (after LTCG tax) proceeds of only $43,250. That's an added benefit of $6,750.

But what if you want to donate the funds to more than one charity and/or you haven't decided just yet where all of the funds are ultimately to go?

The Donor Advised Fund (DAF)

There is an account that can be established that will receive contributions for the benefit of other charitable organizations. It's called a Donor Advised Fund (DAF), and it is available through several foundations. I serve on the board of one such foundation, Christian Foundation of the West (CFW). You can open a DAF account with a contribution of funds (typical minimum is $10,000), and then direct the foundation to make grants to the charities of your choice. You can also allow funds to accumulate for future grants and still get the tax deduction benefits in the current year.

Technically, the funds are no longer yours once you place them into the DAF, thus the immediate tax deduction. You direct the grants of those funds by advising the foundation's board as to the specific charities and amounts. You cannot take any of the funds back out of your DAF for personal use in the future.

The donation of appreciated assets to a foundation with a DAF program offers advantages over gifting directly to the ultimate charity. An asset transfer can fund a Donor Advised Fund and then you, the donor, can recommend grants to the specific charities. By contrast, donating long-term appreciated assets directly to individual charities requires working separately with each of those charities, which may take substantial time and effort. In addition, some charities either do not accept appreciated securities at all or will only consider them for very large donations.

In summary, your contributions to your Donor Advised Fund provide all the tax benefits mentioned above, and the charities of your choosing also benefit tremendously. The capital gains taxes that you would have been paying to the government are forgiven; in addition, you receive the full tax deduction of the amount transferred to the Donor Advised Fund. These added tax savings can increase the amount you have available for even greater generosity.

50% of AGI: Limitation or Wasted Opportunity?

Kay and I attended a weekend conference of The Gathering a few years ago and very much enjoyed a number of testimonies from other couples who were further along in their journey of generosity. We were inspired and challenged. We were also amazed.

One testimony was especially memorable. The wife was the spokesperson for this particular couple, and after briefly sharing the joy of their giving experiences, she proceeded to explain their thoughts about tax planning. She reminded us of the limitation the IRS imposes on the tax deductibility of charitable contributions: 50% of the Adjusted Gross Income (AGI). She also reminded us that if we exceed the 50% limitation, the unused amount can be carried forward to a future tax year and still deducted at that later time. So, no problem if your giving exceeds 50% of your income in a given year. She then warned that if the giving amount is less than 50% of your AGI, the unused amount is not carried forward. Hence, failure to achieve the 50% level in any year would be a wasted opportunity with no possibility of getting it back.

I looked at Kay in disbelief (she was smiling). We were nowhere near 50% in our giving at the time, and I hadn't even considered it as applicable to us in our financial position. Other couples at our table nodded knowingly; I was intimidated and humbled once again. Would there ever be the day when we could seriously contemplate such thinking? I was still trying to digest Ron Blue's earlier suggestion that we give from our assets in addition to giving from our income. So here now was one more thing to contemplate as we moved forward in our giving journey.

By the way, good news on the 50% limitation issue: there is a new provision in the tax law that allows a person over age 70 ½ to allocate some of their IRA accounts for charitable purposes. This can go above and beyond the 50% limitation by up to $100,000 per year. Visit www.WisdomB4Wealth.com for more information on this.

But, what if the tax benefits were taken away?

Hopefully our thinking in reference to tax benefits is only for the purposes of optimizing our cash flows for stewardship purposes. It is unwise to allow the tax tail to wag the dog. In other words, we should not allow tax rules to be the primary reason for any of our actions. We know that the government's intent is to affect taxpayer behavior with these laws, and that's all well and good. But does this mean that if they take away the charitable deduction, we will discontinue our giving? I sure hope not!

There are actually a number of studies concluding that people will make charitable contributions regardless of tax benefits. Over the decades, there have been major changes in tax rates and thus major changes in the tax treatment of charitable contributions. At some points, there have been big tax advantages to giving, at others much less. What is interesting is that charitable giving has averaged about 2% of U.S. gross domestic product regardless of tax rates. [26]

Other countries don't offer write-offs on charitable contributions. There has been pressure to end the charitable deduction in the U.S. because it tends to benefit people in the upper income brackets, who supposedly don't really need it. Upper-income households are the biggest beneficiaries of the deduction, with those making more than $100,000 per year taking 81% of the deduction even though they account for just 13.5% of all U.S. taxpayers.[27] It appears that most people, believers and non-believers alike, will continue to give regardless of the tax benefits. This is a testament to the goodness in people.

Not that I seek the gift, but I seek the fruit that abounds to your account. — **Philippians 4:17 (NKJV)**

We all know that we can't take it with us, but I once heard a funny story of one man who did try to do just that. This man was coming to the end of his days and was concerned about leaving all of his wealth behind.

Every night in his dreams, he prayed to God, "Please, can I take some with me?" God kept saying, "No, that's not how it works."

Finally, God one day relented and said, "You can bring one suitcase with you—that's it."

The man thought he was pretty smart. He filled the suitcase with solid gold bricks. Not long after, he died and showed up at the pearly gates of heaven. Saint Peter looked at the suitcase and asked, "What are you doing? You can't bring anything with you into heaven."

"Actually, God gave me permission to bring just this one suitcase," the man replied.

"Well, okay, let's open it up and see what's inside." The suitcase was opened and after a few eternal seconds, Saint Peter looked up in puzzlement, "You brought pavement?"

Let's face it: the things we have accumulated here on earth will be of little value in heaven. So the idea of taking it with us doesn't really make sense anyway. However, we know that we can send it ahead and multiply it into something meaningful.

> *As for what was sown on good soil, this is the one who hears the word and understands it. He indeed bears fruit and yields, in one case a hundredfold, in another sixty, and in another thirty.* —
> **Matthew 13:23 (ESV)**

This is the message made very clear in Randy Alcorn's book *The Treasure Principle: Unlocking the Secret of Joyful Giving*, in which he introduces readers to a revolution in material freedom and radical generosity.[28] Another inspiring book on this subject is the aforementioned *The Eternity Portfolio* by Alan Gotthardt, in which he presents the groundbreaking framework for intentionally managing your money to invest in God's kingdom.

Financial Freedom

And so we come to realize that achieving financial freedom transcends financial independence. Financial freedom is the ability to hold our wealth with an open hand.

Though there is the natural tendency to think sequentially, financial independence is not a prerequisite to financial freedom. It is reasonable to assume financial independence comes before financial freedom, but this is not necessarily so. We have defined financial independence as the point at which your savings and investments generate enough investment income to meet or exceed your employment income. At this point, work becomes a choice rather than a necessity. However, a person can become financially free even before achieving financial independence. Financial freedom is a function of recognizing God's ownership and developing the joy of generosity.

Once financially independent, then, is it okay to stop saving?

Once you establish the cash-flow priority discipline of paying God first, paying yourself second (saving), and then dealing with the rest, it is difficult to stop saving even once you are already financially independent. I have to admit I still save and invest. Once you have achieved financial freedom and financial independence, it is between you and God as to how you manage the cash flow going forward. Given that we have been allowed to achieve financial independence, there should be a natural tendency to give more generously, and it would seem to be okay to reduce or even stop saving. And of course, it's okay to keep working, but now you are in a position to be "working to give instead of working to live."

First Inclination: Spend, Save, or Give?

During a weekend event put on by the nonprofit organization Generous Giving, I recall a question that our group contemplated: What is your natural inclination when deciding what to do with the receipt of unexpected funds? Some naturally want to spend it. I naturally want to invest it. There were people in my group who naturally wanted to give it. I want to be more like them.

After all, if we're financially independent, why do we work for money? We don't need the money to live. If we've achieved our "how much is enough" goal, then it stands to reason that working increases our capacity to give.

"Contentment Creep"—Is It Bad?

However, while tithing and giving charitably, is it okay to continue increasing your standard of living as well, within reason? A kitchen remodel, a nicer car, a plane—are these wrong to consider when we know that the funds for them could be given to the needy instead?

> *Instruct those who are rich in this present world not to be conceited or to fix their hope on the uncertainty of riches, but on God, who richly supplies us with all things to enjoy.* — *1 Timothy 6:17 (NASB)*

Scripture tells us repeatedly of God's desire to bless us for our enjoyment. Therefore, it would seem that we should enjoy his bountiful blessings in our lives. However, 'moderation' may be the operative word here.

Helping those in need is one of the major themes of the Bible and of Jesus' ministry. As far back as the thirteenth century B.C., the Hebrews' law institutionalized assistance to the poor:

*When you reap the harvest of your land, you shall not reap to the very edges of your field, nor shall you gather the gleanings of your harvest. You shall not strip your vineyard bare, or gather the fallen grapes of your vineyard; you shall leave them for the poor and the alien: I am the LORD your God. — **Leviticus 19:9–10 (NRSV)***

Scripture is not telling you to give away your fields. God has entrusted the fields to you and expects you to be a good steward. There is a balance between immediate giving and allowing your wealth to grow so that you can give more. There should also be a reasonable balance between the enjoyments of an improved lifestyle and increasing your giving. Hopefully, the increase in lifestyle will be in parallel with even greater increases in your giving. Be of one accord with your spouse on this and pray for God's guidance.

Resource Organizations

Next, I'd like to introduce you properly to the aforementioned organization called Generous Giving.

Founded in 2000 by The Maclellan Foundation, Generous Giving's mission is to spread the biblical message of generosity in order to grow generous givers among those entrusted with much. It was launched with a vision to stir a renewed, spirit-led commitment to generosity among followers of Christ through conversation. These conversations consistently allow us and our friends to discover joy in ways we didn't expect.[29]

This is an organization that promotes generous giving, as its name implies. It all started with a few friends. In the late 1990s, giving was at an all-time low. A couple of the founding members noticed and wanted to help reverse this trend. While considering what to do, they began meeting with people they knew who were living radically generous lives. They saw that their lives were marked by the joy, freedom, and fruitfulness that we all crave. They spent time with these generous people, and what they found was that they were inspired simply by having conversations with these men and women. They saw their own paradigms about wealth shifting in beautiful ways. They began to adopt a more generous life naturally.

They began to think, "What if more of us had these conversations? Imagine if others experienced the joy, freedom, and fruitfulness these friends were experiencing. Imagine new family legacies built on generosity with new generations of children growing up with this rich tradition. Imagine all the resources we could free up. Imagine all the good we could do." So they invited more friends into the conversations with them. Presently, the organization offers the following:

Annual celebration of generosity. An experience that brings people from around the country together to consider what it means to be entrusted with wealth, experience the joy of generosity, and excel in the grace of giving.

Small gatherings. An overnight experience with one's peers discussing the generous life. They call these overnight events a Journey of Generosity (JOG) because we are all on our own journeys and it is invaluable to come together to encourage each other along the way. These gatherings are hosted by someone who wants to encourage a conversation about generosity among friends, and they are guided by a Generous Giving facilitator.

Media and resources. Videos, podcasts, and literature are also available via their website at www.generousgiving.org.

Another organization that offers similar resources is The Gathering, a group of individuals, families, and foundations interested in Christian philanthropy. They serve as a resource as well as a source of spiritual encouragement and a sounding board for peers. See TheGathering.com for more information.

Kay and I have been abundantly blessed by both Generous Giving and The Gathering. I urge you to get involved with one or both when the time is right.

Time, Talent, Treasure

While the focus of this book is on finances and possessions (one's treasures), we should also be mindful of the other resources for which we have a stewardship responsibility. As you age, you will come to the realization that time is more valuable than treasures. We can increase treasures, but we cannot increase the time that we have here on this planet. Once spent, it is gone forever.

Nevertheless, an investment of our time into Kingdom purposes will reap rewards for now and in eternity. You will experience joy as you serve others. What a blessing it has been for me to serve at Christian Foundation of the West and in other ministries. What a joy to see our clients become financially independent, achieve financial freedom, and now be free to serve in greater ways than before.

In my youth, I felt guilty about the fact that I didn't sense a call to the mission field or to go into the ministry. But over time, I was comforted by the thought that my role could ultimately be to help finance ministries through generous giving. As an adult, I realized that in addition to giving to established ministries, my daily business activities can serve a ministerial role to the people I meet. A focus on the blessing of our clients, our employees, and our community can be of significant impact on people who perhaps might never attend a church service.

> *For we are his workmanship, created in Christ Jesus unto good works, which God hath beforehand ordained that we should walk in them.* — **Ephesians 2:10 (KJV)**

Good stewardship includes making use of our time, talents, and abilities. We are each blessed with unique talents, and we should put them to good use.

Savor The Moment

A few final words about time; You'll find that life goes by too quickly. The fast pace of today's world causes time to continue accelerating. All too often over the years I failed to live in the moment. Instead my focus was on plans for the future. Planning is good, but not if it denies you the blessing of today, the present. So, a few quick thoughts:

Wherever you are, be there. Be careful when you hear yourself thinking, " I can't wait until this is over." Whatever "this" is (a hard workout, a long drive, a boring lecture in school). Choose instead to enjoy, and even savor every moment. Every today is a gift, so I'll close by encouraging you to enjoy the present.

WORKBOOK

CHAPTER 5 QUESTIONS

Question: How do you invest your time, talent, and treasure in God? How have you experienced God's law of multiplication in your life?

_____

_____

_____

_____

_____

_____

_____

_____

_____

Question: How do you invest your time, talent, and treasure in others? What more could you do?

_____

_____

_____

_____

_____

_____

_____

_____

Question: Where do you get your motivation for giving? What are some of the financial perquisites of giving?

_____

_____

_____

_____

_____

_____

_____

_____

_____

_____

Action: In addition to pursuing financial independence, find true financial freedom by being an effective steward of the money with which God has blessed you—especially by investing in others. No matter your financial status, invest not only your treasure but also your time and talent in God and in other people. Embracing God's math—His law of multiplication—don't hold back, but instead invest proportionally more as your wealth grows. Make sure you're taking advantage of current financial benefits of charitable giving at tax time, but above all, experience and enjoy the growth of real joy in your life.

CHAPTER 5 NOTES

CONCLUSION

"**S**ee You on the Other Side"

Grandparents are a gift from heaven that we often take for granted. I was blessed with four wonderful grandparents. And it seems only fitting to acknowledge them as I conclude this book.

They were immigrants from Italy. They first settled in New Britain, Connecticut, and in Milwaukee, Wisconsin; then they made their way to Los Angeles, California. They took a big risk coming to America, a strange new world of opportunity that was mostly unknown to them. Today, I am living the dream they had for their grandchildren. The risk they took paid off, and I am so thankful to them!

Grandpa Joseph Ferrara was a foundry worker, and Grandma was a homemaker. They were simple, honest, hardworking immigrants. They impacted my life in so many ways. I owe much of who I am today to their wise teachings.

Grandma Isabelle Ferrara was a typical Italian grandmother. She was a big woman, always wearing an apron, stockings rolled to a little past her ankles. Like many women of her time, she always had her hair up in a bun. Being an

Italian grandmother, of course she had the best spaghetti and meatballs!

Grandma was a prayer warrior. I knew she was praying for me all the time. To this day, I carry with me a little cloth that she anointed in oil and gave to me. When I bought my first airplane, she asked to come out to the airport to see it. When we arrived at the parked plane, before I knew it, she had her hands on the propeller, and she prayed over that plane and my future journeys.

Grandma Ferrara was an incredible teacher to me and others. She was the one who taught me about compound interest and also about tithing. A Sunday school teacher for many years, she would brighten the room whenever she entered, and she would always end her Sunday school class by saying, "And remember, if you encounter someone without a smile, give them one of yours."

I remember going to visit her at a very early age. When she would tuck me in bed at night, she would always say, "You cannot comprehend how much I love you. You think you know, but until you are a grandparent, you will simply be unable to understand the magnitude of the love that I have for you." No doubt this is how my mother, Fran, learned about unconditional love, which she too imparted to me and my siblings (Rick, Janet and Judy).

Grandpa Ferrara was my role model for work ethic. I remember watching him walk down the street in the early morning fog, lunch pail in hand as he headed to the foundry in Los Angeles. When he retired and moved to the Palm Springs area, he rose early every morning while it was still dark to tend to his garden. He also had time for my brother and me, taking us on walks in the desert, imparting a few words of wisdom along the way.

For his part, Grandpa Vincent Sanada was my first example of morning devotions. I remember visiting them and getting up early to find him on his knees in the living room, praying and reading his Bible. That is now how I start my mornings, thanks in part to his example.

Grandma Elvera Sanada spoke of heaven to me. In fact, her last words to me, other than I love you, were "I'll see you on the other side." She and my dad, Vincent Sanada, Jr. were my greatest examples of confidence in eternity. It is that same confidence that I hope to impart to you in this conclusion. I trust that with God's wisdom you will steward His wealth and create for yourself an eternity of many great rewards. And with that, my dear ones, I'll see you on the other side.

Appendices:
Doing the Math

Appendix 1

Earning Interest

There is a lot written in the Bible about lending and earning interest:

> *Well then, you should have put my money on deposit with the bankers, so that when I returned I would have received it back with interest.* — **Matthew 25:27 (ESV)**

> *They are always generous and lend freely; their children will be a blessing.* — **Psalm 37:26 (ESV)**

> *It is well with the man who is gracious and lends; He will maintain his cause in judgment.* — **Psalm 112:5 (NASB)**

The Bible does speak about lending money in a positive light, but it also warns us not to make money on lending to the poor. In recent years, modern financial institutions became bloated and financially unstable by making housing loans to people who had no means of paying them back. These toxic loans brought down the housing and lending industries, not to mention the people to whom these loans were made. A lot of grief could have been avoided if biblical principles had been followed in these lending transactions.

The Bible speaks of our lending freely, but it warns us against being greedy. We need to be reasonable. We need to earn a fair rate of return without taking advantage of the poor. There are even times when we should not charge interest:

> *If you lend money to any of my people with you who is poor, you shall not be like a moneylender to him, and you shall not exact interest from him. — **Exodus 22:25 (ESV)***

We need to seek God's wisdom when lending and generating income from our investments, we need to make sure we are deploying our assets with a kind heart. Are you investing your assets to generate a fair return? Are you charging a reasonable interest rate? Is the borrower able or likely to repay? Will this improve their situation? I do believe it is possible for a Christian to lend money, earn interest, and invest his assets to generate income while still being a blessing to all parties in the arrangement.

The Math

If you loan money to an individual or an institution at a stated interest rate, you should expect the receipt of that interest at regular intervals in addition to the repayment of your principal in accordance with the loan agreement. For example, if you loan $12,000 at 10% (annual rate, interest-only, payable monthly) for a period of one year, you will receive $100 in interest each month. Then, at the end of the year, you will receive the $12,000 principal back as well. The total amount received is therefore $13,200.

If instead the loan is "amortized," you will receive interest and principal payments each month instead of a lump sum at the end of the year. The monthly payments will be $1,054.99. Total amount received: $12,659.88.

At first glance, you might wonder why it is that the total received in an amortized loan is less than that from an interest-only loan. The answer lies in the fact that you are receiving your principal back sooner and thus cannot continue charging interest on the amount that has been repaid. Following is an amortization schedule:

Payment	Principal	Interest	Total Interest	Balance
				$12,000.00
$1,054.99	$954.99	$100.00	$100.00	$11,045.01
$1,054.99	$962.95	$92.04	$192.04	$10,082.06
$1,054.99	$970.97	$84.02	$276.06	$9,111.09
$1,054.99	$979.06	$75.93	$351.98	$8,132.02
$1,054.99	$987.22	$67.77	$419.75	$7,144.80
$1,054.99	$995.45	$59.54	$479.29	$6,149.35
$1,054.99	$1,003.75	$51.24	$530.54	$5,145.61
$1,054.99	$1,012.11	$42.88	$573.42	$4,133.50
$1,054.99	$1,020.54	$34.45	$607.86	$3,112.95
$1,054.99	$1,029.05	$25.94	$633.80	$2,083.90
$1,054.99	$1,037.62	$17.37	$651.17	$1,046.28
$1,054.99	$1,046.28	$8.71	$659.88	$(0.00)
$12,659.88	$12,000.00	$659.88		

As you can see, the remaining principal balance declines each month and thus the amount of interest received is reduced.

Appendix 2

Compound Interest
Scripture makes it clear that God expects us to profitably manage the resources He has entrusted to us. He expects us to grow those resources, as we read in the following scriptures:

> *Precious treasure and oil are in a wise man's dwelling, but a foolish man devours it.* — **Proverbs 21:20 (ESV)**

> *The plans of the diligent lead surely to abundance, but everyone who is hasty comes only to poverty.* — **Proverbs 21:5 (ESV)**

The Math
When the interest is not paid out but is instead reinvested, then that reinvested amount should be added to the principal so that during the next period, interest earnings can be received on the new higher balance. This is referred to as compound interest. So if we loan $12,000 at 10% to be compounded monthly, the value of the account at the end of the year would be $13,256.56.

This amount is higher than either of the above two examples because you are now earning interest on interest—compound interest. Following is the schedule that illustrates the growth of the account over the twelve months:

Month	Year	Monthly Interest	Balance
			$12,000.00
1	1	$100.00	$12,100.00
2	1	$100.83	$12,200.83
3	1	$101.67	$12,302.51
4	1	$102.52	$12,405.03
5	1	$103.38	$12,508.40
6	1	$104.24	$12,612.64
7	1	$105.11	$12,717.75
8	1	$105.98	$12,823.73
9	1	$106.86	$12,930.59
10	1	$107.75	$13,038.35
11	1	$108.65	$13,147.00
12	1	$109.56	$13,256.56

So as you can see, when interest is allowed to compound, investment earnings can increase. Not much if for only a year, but look what happens to this same $12,000 account if allowed to compound over 35 years:

Initial investment: **$12,000**

Interest rate: **10%**

Year	Interest	Additional Investment	Accumulated Value
1	$1,200.00	$ ---	$ 13,200.00
2	$1,320.00	$0.00	$ 14,520.00
3	$1,452.00	$0.00	$ 15,972.00
4	$1,597.20	$0.00	$ 17,569.20
5	$1,756.92	$0.00	$ 19,326.12

6	$1,932.61	$0.00	$	21,258.73
7	$2,125.87	$0.00	$	23,384.61
8	$2,338.46	$0.00	$	25,723.07
9	$2,572.31	$0.00	$	28,295.37
10	$2,829.54	$0.00	$	31,124.91
11	$3,112.49	$0.00	$	34,237.40
12	$3,423.74	$0.00	$	37,661.14
13	$3,766.11	$0.00	$	41,427.25
14	$4,142.73	$0.00	$	45,569.98
15	$4,557.00	$0.00	$	50,126.98
16	$5,012.70	$0.00	$	55,139.68
17	$5,513.97	$0.00	$	60,653.64
18	$6,065.36	$0.00	$	66,719.01
19	$6,671.90	$0.00	$	73,390.91
20	$7,339.09	$0.00	$	80,730.00
21	$8,073.00	$0.00	$	88,803.00
22	$8,880.30	$0.00	$	97,683.30
23	$9,768.33	$0.00	$	107,451.63
24	$10,745.16	$0.00	$	118,196.79
25	$11,819.68	$0.00	$	130,016.47
26	$13,001.65	$0.00	$	143,018.12
27	$14,301.81	$0.00	$	157,319.93
28	$15,731.99	$0.00	$	173,051.92
29	$17,305.19	$0.00	$	190,357.12
30	$19,035.71	$0.00	$	209,392.83
31	$20,939.28	$0.00	$	230,332.11
32	$23,033.21	$0.00	$	253,365.32
33	$25,336.53	$0.00	$	278,701.85
34	$27,870.19	$0.00	$	306,572.04
35	$30,657.20	$0.00	$	337,229.24

Wow—$12,000 grows to $337,229 when allowed to compound (annually)!

Now look at the table on the next page and see what happens if you add $1,000 per month to the account.

Notice what happens in year 8: the account grows from $137,231 to $162,954. That's an increase of $25,723. Part of that growth is a function of your $12,000 annual investment. Note, however, that this is the year when your investment account adds more back to itself than you do! Interest earnings that year were $13,723.

Notice also that after 35 years, there is over $3.5 million in the account; the investment is now generating over $325,000 each year in interest earnings.

Initial investment			$12,000
Interest rate			10%
Year	Interest	Additional Investment	Accumulated Value
1	$1,200.00	$12,000.00	$25,200.00
2	$2,520.00	$12,000.00	$39,720.00
3	$3,972.00	$12,000.00	$55,692.00
4	$5,569.20	$12,000.00	$73,261.20
5	$7,326.12	$12,000.00	$92,587.32
6	$9,258.73	$12,000.00	$113,846.05
7	$11,384.61	$12,000.00	$137,230.66
8	$13,723.07	$12,000.00	$162,953.72
9	$16,295.37	$12,000.00	$191,249.10
10	$19,124.91	$12,000.00	$222,374.00
11	$22,237.40	$12,000.00	$256,611.41
12	$25,661.14	$12,000.00	$294,272.55
13	$29,427.25	$12,000.00	$335,699.80
14	$33,569.98	$12,000.00	$381,269.78
15	$38,126.98	$12,000.00	$431,396.76
16	$43,139.68	$12,000.00	$486,536.43
17	$48,653.64	$12,000.00	$547,190.08
18	$54,719.01	$12,000.00	$613,909.09
19	$61,390.91	$12,000.00	$687,299.99
20	$68,730.00	$12,000.00	$768,029.99
21	$76,803.00	$12,000.00	$856,832.99
22	$85,683.30	$12,000.00	$954,516.29
23	$95,451.63	$12,000.00	$1,061,967.92
24	$106.196.79	$12,000.00	$1,180,164.71
25	$118,016.47	$12,000.00	$1,310,181.18
26	$131,018.12	$12,000.00	$1,453,199.30
27	$145,319.93	$12,000.00	$1,610,519.23
28	$161,051.92	$12,000.00	$1,783,571.16
29	$178,357.12	$12,000.00	$1,973,928.27
30	$197,392.83	$12,000.00	$2,183,321.10
31	$218,332.11	$12,000.00	$2,413,653.21
32	$241,365.32	$12,000.00	$2,667,018.53
33	$266,701.85	$12,000.00	$2,945,720.38
34	$294,572.04	$12,000.00	$3,252,292.42
35	$325,229.24	$12,000.00	$3,589,521.66

The Parable of the Talents

For it will be like a man going on a journey, who called his servants and entrusted to them his property. To one he gave five talents, to another two, to another one, to each according to his ability. Then he went away. He who had received the five talents went at once and traded with them, and he made five talents more. So also he who had the two talents made two talents more. But he who had received the one talent went and dug in the ground and hid his master's money. Now after a long time the master of those servants came and settled accounts with them.

And he who had received the five talents came forward, bringing five talents more, saying, "Master, you delivered to me five talents; here I have made five talents more." His master said to him, "Well done, good and faithful servant. You have been faithful over a little; I will set you over much. Enter into the joy of your master."

And he also who had the two talents came forward, saying, "Master, you delivered to me two talents; here I have made two talents more." His master said to him, "Well done, good and faithful servant. You have been faithful over a little; I will set you over much. Enter into the joy of your master."

He also who had received the one talent came forward, saying, "Master, I knew you to be a hard man, reaping where you did not sow, and gathering where you scattered no seed, so I was afraid, and I went and hid your talent in the ground. Here you have what is yours."

But his master answered him, "You wicked and slothful servant! You knew that I reap where I have not sown and gather where I scattered no seed? Then you ought to have invested my money

with the bankers, and at my coming I should have received what was my own with interest. So take the talent from him and give it to him who has the ten talents. For to everyone who has will more be given, and he will have an abundance. But from the one who has not, even what he has will be taken away. And cast the worthless servant into the outer darkness. In that place there will be weeping and gnashing of teeth.”
—Matthew 25:14–30 (ESV)

Appendix 3

Financial Independence Formulas--Expanded Matrix

How to Use

For example, to find the time (in years) it would take to become financially independent with a savings rate of 20% and an investment yield of 8%:

1. Locate the row for the savings rate which corresponds to the savings rate [20%]
2. Locate the column which corresponds to the investment yield [8%]
3. The year to financial independence is located where the savings rate row meets the investment yield column [24]

Formula 15 is depicted in GRAY

Savings as a Percentage of Income (rows) — *Investment Yield* (columns)

Savings \ Yield	1%	2%	3%	4%	5%	6%	7%	8%	9%	10%	11%	12%	13%	14%	15%	16%	17%	18%
30%	148	75	50	38	31	26	22	20	18	16	15	13	12	12	11	10	10	9
29%	150	76	51	39	31	26	23	20	18	16	15	14	13	12	11	11	10	10
28%	153	77	52	39	32	27	23	20	18	16	15	14	13	12	12	11	10	10
27%	156	79	53	40	32	27	23	21	18	17	15	14	13	13	12	11	11	10
26%	159	80	54	41	33	28	24	21	19	17	16	14	14	13	12	11	11	10
25%	162	82	55	42	33	28	24	21	19	17	16	15	14	13	12	12	11	10
24%	166	83	56	42	34	29	25	22	20	18	16	15	14	13	13	12	11	11
23%	169	85	57	43	35	29	25	22	20	18	17	15	15	13	13	12	12	11
22%	173	87	58	44	36	30	26	23	20	18	17	16	15	14	13	13	12	11
21%	177	89	60	45	36	31	27	23	21	19	17	16	15	14	14	13	12	11
20%	181	91	61	46	37	31	27	24	21	19	18	16	16	14	14	13	12	12
19%	185	93	63	47	38	32	28	24	22	20	18	17	16	15	14	13	13	12
18%	189	95	64	48	39	33	28	25	22	20	19	17	17	15	14	14	13	12
17%	194	98	66	50	40	34	29	26	23	21	19	18	17	16	15	14	13	12
16%	200	101	68	51	41	34	30	26	23	21	20	18	18	16	15	14	14	13
15%	205	103	69	52	42	35	31	27	24	22	20	19	18	16	15	14	14	13
14%	211	106	71	54	43	36	31	28	25	23	21	20	19	17	16	15	15	13
13%	218	110	74	56	45	38	32	29	26	23	22	20	20	18	16	16	15	14
12%	225	113	76	57	46	39	34	30	26	24	22	21	21	18	17	16	15	14
11%	233	117	79	59	48	40	35	31	27	25	23	22	21	19	18	17	16	15
10%	241	122	82	62	50	42	37	32	28	26	24	23	23	20	18	17	16	15
9%	251	126	85	64	52	43	39	34	29	27	25	23	23	21	19	18	17	16
8%	262	132	89	67	54	45	41	36	31	28	27	24	25	22	20	19	18	17
7%	275	138	93	70	56	47	43	38	32	29	28	25	24	22	21	20	19	18
6%	289	146	98	74	59	50	45	40	34	31	30	27	25	24	22	21	20	19
5%	306	154	103	78	63	53	49	43	36	32	30	29	27	25	24	22	21	20
4%	328	165	111	84	67	56	53	46	38	35	32	31	29	27	24	24	22	21
3%	356	179	120	91	73	61	56	49	42	38	34	33	31	29	26	24	23	22
2%	396	199	134	101	81	68	60	52	46	42	38	35	33	31	29	27	26	24
1%	464	234	157	118	95	80	69	60	54	49	45	41	38	36	34	32	30	28

Financial Independence Formulas

Savings as a Percentage of Income (rows) vs. Investment Yield (columns)

Savings ↓ / Yield →	1%	2%	3%	4%	5%	6%	7%	8%	9%	10%	11%	12%	13%	14%	15%	16%	17%	18%
30%	148	75	50	38	31	26	22	20	18	16	15	13	12	12	11	10	10	9
29%	150	76	51	39	31	26	23	20	18	16	15	13	13	12	11	11	10	10
28%	153	77	52	39	32	27	23	20	18	16	15	13	13	12	11	11	10	10
27%	156	79	53	40	32	27	23	21	18	17	15	13	13	12	12	11	10	10
26%	159	80	54	41	33	28	24	21	19	17	16	14	14	13	12	11	11	10
25%	162	82	55	42	33	28	24	22	19	17	16	14	14	13	12	12	11	10
24%	166	83	56	42	34	29	25	22	20	18	16	14	14	13	12	12	11	10
23%	169	85	57	43	35	29	25	23	20	18	17	15	15	14	12	12	11	11
22%	173	87	58	44	36	30	26	23	21	18	17	15	15	14	13	12	12	11
21%	177	89	60	45	36	31	26	24	21	19	17	16	15	14	13	12	12	11
20%	181	91	61	46	37	31	27	24	22	19	18	16	16	15	14	13	12	11
19%	185	93	63	47	38	32	28	25	22	20	18	17	16	15	14	13	12	12
18%	189	95	64	48	39	33	28	25	22	20	19	17	16	16	14	13	12	12
17%	194	98	66	50	40	34	29	26	23	21	19	18	17	16	14	13	13	12
16%	200	101	68	51	41	34	30	26	23	21	19	18	17	16	15	14	13	13
15%	205	103	69	52	42	35	31	27	24	22	20	19	18	17	15	14	13	13
14%	211	106	71	54	43	36	31	28	25	23	21	19	18	17	16	15	14	14
13%	218	110	74	56	45	38	32	29	26	23	21	20	19	18	16	15	14	14
12%	225	113	76	57	46	39	34	30	27	24	22	21	19	18	17	16	15	14
11%	233	117	79	59	48	40	35	31	28	25	23	21	20	18	17	16	15	15
10%	241	122	82	62	50	42	36	32	28	26	23	22	21	20	18	17	16	16
9%	251	126	85	64	52	43	37	33	29	27	24	23	22	21	18	17	16	17
8%	262	132	89	67	54	45	39	34	31	28	25	24	23	22	19	18	17	18
7%	275	138	93	70	56	47	41	36	32	29	28	25	24	23	20	19	18	19
6%	289	146	98	74	59	50	43	38	34	31	30	28	25	24	21	20	19	20
5%	306	154	103	78	63	53	45	40	36	32	32	29	27	25	22	21	20	22
4%	328	165	111	84	67	56	49	43	38	35	34	33	29	27	24	22	21	24
3%	356	179	120	91	73	61	53	46	42	38	36	35	32	29	26	24	23	26
2%	396	199	134	101	81	68	59	52	46	42	38	33	35	31	29	27	26	30
1%	464	234	157	118	95	80	69	60	54	49	45	41	38	36	34	32	30	28

Investment Yield

Appendix 4

Asset Balance Matrix Detail

Following is a full overview of the Asset Balance Matrix for the benefit of both readers and their financial advisors.

The Foundation of Investment Balance

While diversification is important for reducing risk, investment balance has the ability to temper the sacrifice of yield that can result. The objective is to optimize investment yields while minimizing risk exposure; this requires proper balance between different kinds of assets. There are two primary dimensions of balance to be considered. The first dimension addresses conventional investment balance in two broad categories: income assets and growth assets.

INCOME ASSETS (Debt or Lender Assets)	GROWTH ASSETS (Equity or Owner Assets)
Money you "loan" in return for specified interest payments and the eventual return of your principal	Represents "ownership" in the underlying asset with full potential for appreciation and investment earnings

The second dimension of investment balance addresses contemporary investment strategy, which suggests that assets should be divided into three important classes: stable assets, financial assets, and tangible assets (also known as alternative assets).

Stable Assets	Principal remains constant and secure
Financial Assets	Marketable securities with the potential for higher yields
Tangible Assets	Assets with a physical nature

The Asset Balance Matrix®

The blending of these two dimensions results in a dynamic analytical tool: the Asset Balance Matrix® (ABM).

ABM	INCOME ASSETS	GROWTH ASSETS
Stable Assets	Savings Certificates of Deposit Money Market	Index Annuities Index Certificates Index CDs
Financial Assets	Government Bonds Corporate Bonds Municipal Bonds	Stocks Equity Mutual Funds International Securities
Tangible Assets	Mortgage Loans Business Loans Venture Loans	Real Estate Private Placements Alternative Investments

Maintaining investment balance helps reduce the risk of buying high and selling low, a big problem where many people fall prey. The goal instead is to buy low and sell high. Via the balance discipline, we try to harvest gains during times when markets are high (as evidenced by an out of balance condition) and purchase while markets are low.

Fellow financial advisors; please feel free to use this tool in your practice. You can use this and any material within this book to help your clients as you see fit. The trademark is not to prevent others from using it, but rather to protect our rights as to its origins.

So let's go into some detail here, starting with the first dimension of balance—the relationship between income assets and growth assets:

Income assets are those for which you are a lender. These assets include savings accounts, T-bills, money market accounts, and bonds, by which you are loaning money to corporations or governments. Also included are mortgages, where you are loaning on someone else's home or commercial property as collateral. These are all areas where someone else is using your money for their investment purposes and paying you interest for the use of your funds.

Growth assets represent actual ownership or equity in the particular business, whether it be ownership of stocks (which is ownership of a corporation) or direct ownership in a small business. Ownership in real estate as an investment is another example, one where all the profitability accrues to you as the owner. You get all the benefits, but you're now subject to all the risks. That's why it's appropriate to have a reasonable balance between income assets and growth assets.

"Proper balance" doesn't necessarily mean 50/50. The appropriate balance is based on one's risk tolerance, cash reserve requirements, cash flow requirements, age, and proximity to retirement. These are all considerations that help determine the correct balance for a given individual.

Let's pause and contemplate this discipline for a moment. If we maintain balance, even on just this single dimension, we will find that it helps us avoid the "buy high and sell low" syndrome.

The number one investment strategy we all know about is "buy low, sell high." Everyone knows that's what you're supposed to do—buy low and sell high. What do you suppose most people do? They do the opposite.

We are all subject to the emotions of greed and fear. When the markets are flying high, greed kicks in. People want to buy. Then when the market drops, what are we tempted to do? We typically want to sell. Emotions of fear are kicking in and we want to get out. People often have a hard time overcoming these emotions, and as a result, the typical investment performance for individual investors lags the market by 3.5% on average.[30] Chasing performance by selling during panicky times and buying during giddy times contributes significantly to this statistic.

So how is it that investment balance can help here? For purposes of demonstration, let's consider a 50/50 balance of a $1 million investment portfolio in stocks and bonds. So we buy a $500,000 portfolio of stocks, and a $500,000 portfolio of bonds, and we give it a year. Sure enough, the growth assets don't grow. Instead the stocks go from $500,000 to $400,000—a 20% decline in a year's time (which happens now and then).

For purposes of this example, assume the bonds also did relatively poorly, with no increase or decrease. Now you have $400,000 on the growth side (in stocks) and $500,000 still on the income side (in bonds). The portfolio total is now $900,000. What are you going to do at the end of that period when it's time to rebalance? Many people would say, "Well, stocks are terrible. Let's sell the stocks and buy more bonds, which appear to be safe." That would be unwise.

The discipline of maintaining balance means that you would transfer $50,000 of the bonds over to the stocks. Now you have $450,000 on each side—back to the 50/50 targeted balance. At a later time assuming the stock market recovers and the value of your stocks goes up by $112,500 (note, recovering from a 20% decline produces a 25% increase), your portfolio now totals $1,012,500 (assuming the bonds had another period of no change). So the recovery of the stocks resulted in a $12,500 overall gain (rather than just breaking even) due to the earlier rebalancing.

By maintaining the balance discipline, you have avoided the buy high, sell low syndrome. Instead, you enjoyed a gain during a couple periods where the markets actually made no progress. In fact the balance discipline caused you to buy low while the stocks were at a discounted value. Likewise, when the stock market later climbs further and it comes time to rebalance again, you will now harvest a portion of those gains (thus sell high) and move them over to the bonds.

Note, you're not timing the market. Nobody has the ability to predict market tops and bottoms accurately. With investment rebalancing, you're not necessarily going to hit those absolute peaks or bottoms. The intent is for selling to occur in the higher market *ranges* and buying in the lower market *ranges*.

You'll want to rebalance at regular intervals, typically once every six months to a year. The asset balance concept is actually quite simple, easy to understand and execute. There's potential to enhance returns via the balance discipline thereby helping offset the dilutive effects of diversification.

So that's the first dimension of investment balance: the relationship between income and growth assets. Because we're discussing a matrix, let's complete it by addressing the second dimension, which is the relationship between stable assets, financial assets, and tangible assets. Here we are looking at the same assets, but from a different perspective.

Stable assets are those for which the principal doesn't fluctuate—for example, a passbook savings account or a money market account. Money in the stable category doesn't produce much in the way of investment yield. For example, if you invest $10,000 in stable assets today, a year from now it will be worth $10,000, plus a few pennies of interest. Unfortunately, today stable assets pay very little (if any) interest. Yet it's an important component to use because we need reserves for everyday needs, for emergencies, and for opportunities. By the way, stable assets are generally quite liquid, meaning you can draw money from them with little or no delay. Passbook and money market accounts, for example, are liquid daily.

The next category is **financial assets**, which are typically stocks, bonds, and mutual funds—investments traded on the financial markets. Here you can earn better dividends and interest, typically in excess of what you receive in the stable assets. You also have the potential for market appreciation. As the various financial markets climb, the value of your mutual fund increases. As the markets decline, so will your mutual fund. Essentially, your financial assets will fluctuate with the supply and demand pressures of the financial markets. Over the long run, you will typically average better returns in financial assets than in stable assets, but you do so with a roller coaster experience along the way.

Finally, **tangible assets** are investments of a physical nature: business equipment, real estate investment properties, collectables, natural resources, direct investment in a private business, etc. Tangible assets can offer some of the highest investment returns, but they come with additional risk exposures. First, they are typically very illiquid—you can't sell off a piece of real estate to raise a little cash for your vacation next week. Most tangible assets take some time to liquidate, and costs are typically incurred in the process of selling.

Tangible assets are often "leveraged," meaning that they are purchased with a combination of cash and debt. Debt means added risk, because if the income from the asset is insufficient to make the payments on that debt, you will have to come up with the funds elsewhere or you will lose the asset, which was the collateral on that debt. Tangible assets are typically not appropriate in the early phase of your wealth accumulation. Considerable reserves should be in place first. Also, most tangible assets are offered only to "accredited" investors, those with over $1 million in net worth, exclusive of the equity in their home. (See the website www.WisdomB4Wealth.com for details on accredited attributes.)

Thus, balance between the three categories—stable assets, financial assets, and tangible assets—is important here in the second dimension of investment balance. Balance need not translate to 33.3% in each category, but rather a balance that is appropriate to the individual based on age, risk propensity, reserve requirements, etc.

There is a third dimension I'll touch on only briefly. It addresses the diversification within each category of the Asset Balance Matrix. For example, the stock and bond markets are composed of numerous styles and sectors (e.g., large-cap value stocks, small-cap growth stocks, government bonds, etc.). You should work with your investment advisor to diversify your portfolio *within* and *across* these asset classes.

Dimension III

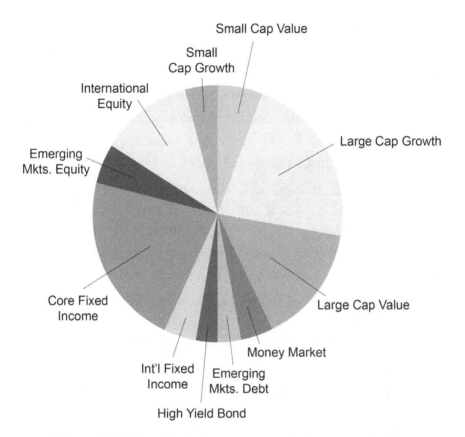

Like diversification, investment balance can have a somewhat dilutive effect on investment returns (especially when rebalancing doesn't occur). Also, history shows that a buy and hold strategy with a high concentration of growth assets has delivered superior returns over the long term (see appendix 6 for the Dow and S&P 500 stock charts). Or if you're exceptionally lucky, you'll place a major investment in a start-up dot.com that makes it big, like Amazon or FaceBook. No doubt you've read at least one story about someone who struck it rich on one amazing opportunity in which they had placed most of their money. But the editors often don't bother to include the stories of the other 99% of individuals, who tried the same thing and lost it all.

Don't make the mistake of thinking that you can predict the future when it comes to investment markets. Many have proposed methods offering to predict what the markets were going to do, without consistent success. I have never found any formula or any person that can consistently predict where the markets are going to go. It just isn't possible— there are too many random and uncontrollable factors. For us to think that we can start doing so now is foolhardy. I've also found that when left to their own devices (without wise counsel and without a discipline like the ABM) most people will eventually succumb to the buy high, sell low syndrome. Maintaining the discipline of investment balance is the way to prepare for and benefit from market fluctuations. So whatever the markets do, we have a plan—we're going to stay balanced.

You should note that the Asset Balance Matrix* applies to your investment portfolio, not your personal assets. While your home is a real estate asset, it's not investment real estate. Thus, don't include your home value into the Asset Balance Matrix. It's appropriate to include it as part of your net worth, of course, and hopefully you'll make money on it over the years. However, when you eventually sell your home, what are you going to do with the proceeds? Buy another home? You have to live someplace. Only on rare occasions might someone sell their home because they're now going to live in a smaller house or a retirement community and will actually have some of the sale proceeds to add to their investment portfolio. The point here is that your residence is used primarily for consumption purposes.

Another consideration is one's private business. This also is not part of your Asset Balance Matrix˙. By the way, one of the best investments you can make is in your own business. However, it should not be your only investment. You should have an investment portfolio above and beyond your business. In other words, don't put all your eggs in the business basket.

Set up a pension or retirement plan, have savings and reserves besides your business savings, and have tangible assets. Invest in other people's businesses, too, where they can work and grow your financial independence portfolio. These all are parts of your Asset Balance Matrix, whereas your personal business is not.

Appendix 5

Dollar Cost Averaging – Game #2

In the text, we played a little game together to learn about dollar cost averaging (DCA). Following is another game that will test your understanding. In this game, you will select from one of four investment options. Once again, you will have the benefit of knowing in advance all of the purchase prices and the final sale price of your shares. Below are the figures.

Invest $1,000 per period:

A	SHARES	B	C	D
$380	2.63	$380	$380	$380
$400	2.50	$360	$80	$460
$420	____	$340	$50	$500
$440	____	$320	$100	$580
$460	____	$300	$190	$420
	X$460			
	$-5,000			
	=____			

What you see above is the price per share for each period for each investment option. So, for example, if you were to choose Investment A, you would invest $1,000 in the first period at a price of $380 per share, meaning that you would purchase 2.63 shares ($1,000÷380 = 2.63). In the second period, you would invest another $1,000 at a price of $400 per share and thus acquire 2.5 shares. You would repeat the process each period until period five, when you would make your final purchase at a price of $460. You would then sell all of your shares at the fifth period's price of $460. To calculate your gains or losses, you would then subtract your total investment amount of $5,000 from the total sale proceeds.

Okay, now it's time to make your choice. Before looking ahead, choose Investment A, Investment B, Investment C, or Investment D.

Now look at the calculated results:

A		B		C		D	
$380	2.63	$380	2.63	$380	2.63	$380	2.63
$400	2.50	$360	2.78	$80	12.50	$460	2.17
$420	2.38	$340	2.94	$50	20.00	$500	2.00
$440	2.27	$320	3.13	$100	10.00	$580	1.72
$460	2.17	$300	3.33	$190	5.26	$420	2.38
	11.95		14.81		50.39		10.90
	X $460		X $300		X $190		X $420
	=5,499		=4,443		=9,574		=4,578
	$-5,000		$-5,000		$-5,000		$-5,000
	$499 Gain		$<557> Loss		$4,574 Gain		$<422> Loss

If you are like most people, you probably chose Investment A because it looked safe. And it was, while generating a modest gain of $499. Investment C is typically the least chosen option, and understandably so at first glance because the ending price was at only half of the starting price. And yet it was somehow the most profitable. This once again is due to the phenomenon produced by dollar cost averaging (DCA), whereby a larger proportion of shares is purchased during the periods when prices are low. This also causes the average *cost* per share purchased to be lower than the average *price* per share.

As in the case of the DCA example in the text, we must acknowledge that such wide variations in share prices are highly unusual when considering a balanced portfolio that reflects the American economy. However, in this particular case, we are in fact looking at our own history. Investment C is actually the Dow Jones Industrial on selected days during the Depression years of 1929, 1931, 1933, 1935, and 1937. It's interesting to note that while the gain for Investment C was $4574 in 1937 with the Dow at 190, the Dow later reached 1,000 in 1972 and now is around 24,000. At that price level, those same 50.39 shares that cost $5,000 would be worth $1.2 million today, in 2017.

Appendix 6

Dow Jones and S&P 500 Stock Charts

Dow Jones
12/1986 - 12/2016

S&P 500

12/1986 - 12/2016

Appendix 7

Cost of Waiting One Year

It is so easy to say "I will start my IRA next year." When we say this, we assume that our one-year delay is no big deal— it's just one of 35 years. "I'll only be giving up 1/35 of my future retirement account." Not true. When we put off starting investments, it has a profound effect on our future.

Look at the table on the next page. While 1/35 of the retirement fund after 35 years is $46,848 ($1,639,697 ÷ 35), the actual cost of waiting one year is $154,563 ($1,639,697 − $1,485,134).

Cost of Waiting One Year

Year	Beginning Balance & investment	% Return	Earning	Ending Balance
1	$5,500	10%	$550	$6,050
2	$11,550	10%	$1,155	$12,705
3	$18,205	10%	$1,821	$20,026
4	$25,526	10%	$2,553	$28,078
5	$33,578	10%	$3,358	$36,936
6	$42,436	10%	$4,244	$46,679
7	$52,179	10%	$5,218	$57,397
8	$62,897	10%	$6,290	$69,187
9	$74,687	10%	$7,469	$82,156
10	$87,656	10%	$8,766	$96,421
11	$101,921	10%	$10,192	$112,114
12	$117,614	10%	$11,761	$129,375
13	$134,875	10%	$13,487	$148,362
14	$153,862	10%	$15,386	$169,249
15	$174,749	10%	$17,475	$192,224
16	$197,724	10%	$19,772	$217,496
17	$222,996	10%	$22,300	$245,295
18	$250,795	10%	$25,080	$275,875
19	$281,375	10%	$28,137	$309,512
20	$315,012	10%	$31,501	$346,514
21	$352,014	10%	$35,201	$387,215
22	$392,715	10%	$39,272	$431,987
23	$437,487	10%	$43,749	$481,235
24	$486,735	10%	$48,674	$535,409
25	$540,909	10%	$54,091	$595,000
26	$600,500	10%	$60,050	$660,550
27	$666,050	10%	$66,605	$732,655
28	$738,155	10%	$73,815	$811,970
29	$817,470	10%	$81,747	$899,217
30	$904,717	10%	$90,472	$995,189
31	$1,000,689	10%	$100,069	$1,100,758
32	$1,106,258	10%	$110,626	$1,216,883
33	$1,222,383	10%	$122,238	$1,344,622
34	$1,350,122	10%	$135,012	$1,485,134
35	$1,490,634	10%	$149,063	$1,639,697

NOTES

1. Pous, Terri. "The Stories of the Lottery's Unluckiest Winners." 27 November 2012. *Time*. Time Inc. http://newsfeed.time.com/2012/11/28/500-million-powerball-jackpot-the-tragic-stories-of-the-lotterys-unluckiest-winners/slide/andrew-jack-whittaker/.

2. Kates, Ann. "5 Strategies to Keep Your Heirs from Blowing Their Inheritance." *Kiplinger's Personal Finance*. Nov. 2015. In *Kiplinger.com*. The Kiplinger Washington Editors. http://www.kiplinger.com/article/saving/T021-C000-S002-5-strategies-keep-heirs-from-blowing-inheritance.html.

3. *Ibid*.

4. *Ibid*.

5. "4907. sunesis." From *Thayer's Greek Lexicon*, Electronic Database, Biblesoft, Inc., 2011. *Bible Hub*. http://biblehub.com/greek/4907.htm

6. Bouchard, M., and McGue, T. J., Jr. "Familial Studies of Intelligence: A Review." *Science* 212 (1981): 1055—9.

7. Plomin, R., DeFries, J. C., McClearn, G. E., and Rutter, M. *Behavioral Genetics* (3rd ed.) (Freeman, 1997).

8. DiLalla, L. F. "Development of Intelligence: Current Research and Theories." *Journal of School Psychology* 38, no. 1 (2000). https://www.researchgate.net/publication/234691150_Development_of_Intelligence_Current_Research_and_Theories.

9. "4678. sophia." From *Strong's Concordance. Bible Hub.* http://biblehub.com/greek/4678.htm

10. Waltke, Bruce K. *The Book of Proverbs: Chapters 1–15* (Eerdmans, 2004), 77—8.

11. *Merriam-Webster*, online ed., s.v. "Discipline." https://www.merriam-webster.com/dictionary/discipline.

12. *Merriam-Webster*, online ed., s.v. "Self-discipline." https://www.merriam-webster.com/dictionary/self-discipline.

13. "Designation." *Kingdom Advisors.* https://www.kingdomadvisors.com/association/designation.

14. "Compass Map." *Compass—Finances God's Way.* Image. http://compass1.org/resources/compass-map/

15. Through December 2016. *Bloomberg Barclays U.S. Aggregate Bond Index.* Standard & Poors Index Services group.

16. Andersen, Peter. "What's Better: Lump Sum Investing or Dollar Cost Averaging?" *Forbes.* http://www.forbes.com/sites/investor/2015/11/17/whats-better-lump-sum-investing-or-dollar-cost-averaging/#481f6e2563b7.

17. Kiersz, Andy. "The Best Way to Buy Stocks Is to Go All In and Wait." *Business Insider*. http://www.businessinsider.com/lump-sum-vs-dollar-cost-averaging-2014-12.

18. Blue, Ron. *Master Your Money: A Step-by-Step Plan for Financial Freedom* (rev. ed.) (Thomas Nelson, 1991).

19. Dayton, Howard. *Your Money Counts* (reprint) (Thomas Nelson, 2011).

20. Phelps, Glenn, and Crabtree, Steven. "Worldwide, Median Household Income about $10,000." *Gallup*. http://www.gallup.com/poll/166211/worldwide-median-household-income-000.aspx?.

21. Steverman, Ben. "Two-Thirds of Americans Aren't Putting Money in Their 401(k)." *Financial Advisor*. Charter Financial Publishing Network. 21 February 2017. http://www.fa-mag.com/news/two-thirds-of-americans-aren-t-putting-money-in-their-401-k-31449.html?section=43

22. Rehurek, Jon. "Non-Negotiables of Credit Card Use." In *Biblical Stewardship of Money*. Fall 2015 syllabus. Logos Bible Institute, Grace Community Church, Sun Valley, CA. 61–63.

23. Nightingale, Earl. "The Strangest Secret, Earl Nightingale 1950 (with Subtitles)." YouTube video. https://www.youtube.com/watch?v=5sloRyDg1pM.

24. Hobbs, Diana. "Content but Not Complacent." *Your Daily Cup of Inspiration*. 16 October 2008. http://www.diannahobbs.com/dianna_hobbs_empowering_e/2008/10/content-but-not-complacent.html

25. Gotthardt, Alan. *The Eternity Portfolio* (Tyndale House, 2003).

26. "Should We End the Tax Deduction for Charitable Donations?" *Wall Street Journal*. 16 December 2012. http://www.wsj.com/articles/SB1000142412788732446 93045781433514706610998.

27. Duquette, Nicholas J. "Do Tax Incentives Affect Charitable Contributions? Evidence from Public Charities' Reported Revenues." University of Southern California, 2014. https://bedrosian.usc.edu/files/2015/05/Duquette-Do-Tax-Incentives-Affect-Charitable-Contributions-Evidence-from-Public-Charities-Reported-Revenues.pdf

28. Alcorn, Randy. *The Treasure Principle: Unlocking the Secret of Joyful Giving* (Multnomah, 2001).

29. "We Are Committed to Spreading the Biblical Message of Generosity." *Generous Giving*. https://generousgiving.org/who-we-are#about-us.

30. "Quantitative Analysis of Investor Behavior." *Dalbar*. From *Wall Street Journal* (weekend ed.), 7–8 May 2016, B12. https://www.qaib.com/public/about

INDEX

ABOUT THE AUTHOR

Having achieved financial independence at an early age, Randall retired from his full-time role as a financial advisor at IDS American Express.

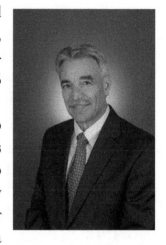

He opened a family office in 1987 to manage his family investment holdings and accommodated other families who wanted to do likewise. The multifamily office was named Alliance, and a broker dealer was purchased. Ultimately, a bank and trust company was formed in partnership with some other investment advisory firms.

Randall's two oldest sons, Randy Jr., and Jerry now run the investment advisory side of the firm as well as most of the subsidiary companies that have evolved. Randall continues with the firm as a sounding board for his sons and to aid in the due diligence work associated with the acquisition of new investment opportunities.

His time is now devoted to ministry endeavors. Randall was a founding member of Kingdom Advisors with

Larry Burkett and Ron Blue. He's also chairman of the board at Christian Foundation of the West. He also serves on the board of the Kingdom Centers which provides housing for widows and orphans.

Randall holds two Bachelor of Science degrees:
  Business Management and *Data Processing*
Two Master of Science degrees:
  Financial Services (MSFS) and *Management (MSM)*
And the following professional designations:
  CFP* – *Certified Financial Planner*
  CLU – *Chartered Life Underwriter*
  ChFC – *Chartered Financial Consultant*
  CKA* – *Certified Kingdom Advisor*®

Randall enjoys snow skiing, flying aircraft, and driving race cars with his four sons and four grandchildren—and entertaining with his bride, Kay, to whom he's been married since 1972.

**For more information
or to connect with the author:**
See: www.wb4w.org
www.facebook.com/wisdombeforewealth
Or write to: info@wb4w.org

CPSIA information can be obtained
at www.ICGtesting.com
Printed in the USA
LVHW031348151118
596830LV00006B/170/P

9 781946 453044